By the sar

Tsunami Days
observations

John Barnie

LEAF BY LEAF

Published by Leaf by Leaf
an imprint of Cinnamon Press,
Office 49019, PO Box 92, Cardiff, CF11 1NB
www.cinnamonpress.com
The right of John Barnie to be identified as author of this work has been
asserted by him in accordance with the Copyright, Designs and Patent
Act, 1988. © 2023 John Barnie
Print Edition ISBN 978-1-78864-985-8

Designed and typeset in Adobe Caslon Pro by Cinnamon Press.
Cover design by Adam Craig © Adam Craig.
Picture credits: ice cube: unalozmen/istockphoto; noise: Sohl/istockphoto
Cinnamon Press is represented by Inpress.

Acknowledgements

Some of these observations first appeared in *The New Welsh Review*
and *O'r Pedwar Gwynt,* and on the Sustainable Wales website.

CONTENTS

Everything has changed except our way of thinking
Albert Einstein

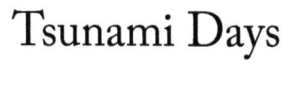

Tsunami Days

Foreword

These short essays are an attempt to understand what is happening to humanity and the Earth amid the huge confusion of our times. It seems to me that we cannot do this adequately without knowing something of the way our species evolved within the deeper structure of the genus *Homo* over the past two million years.

We need to understand the limitations evolution has placed on the human brain, remarkable though it is, if we are to formulate an adequate response to the multiple and interconnected global catastrophes we have inadvertently set in motion. We can formulate responses to this at an intellectual level; the great and pressing question is whether our brain is sufficiently advanced to allow us to transform perception into practice, to change radically our way of living, not in twenty, thirty, or forty years, but *now*, and to do this co-operatively on a global scale.

This is one thread in these 'observations' which are interspersed with personal reflections and comment on more specific aspects of culture and society.

My view is pessimistic, because the situation is far worse than most people are willing to believe. As a consequence, there will be readers who won't like what I say; who will object that 'human ingenuity will always find a way'.

Perhaps they are right, but if they are wrong and I am right, what then?

Delight in Killing

In a recent issue of the *NYRB* there is a review of a book of Martha Gellhorn's letters. Accompanying it is a photograph of Gellhorn wading through a vast acreage of wheat in Idaho, taken in 1940. She is cradling a double-barrelled shotgun and looks defiantly, so it seems, toward the camera—the great chronicler of the horror and pity of war setting out to shoot whatever creatures she can find crouched in the wheat.

I have another cutting of the Eagle Hunt Club, taken in a forest clearing in Poland. A dozen burley men, shotguns shouldered, are walking away from a wooden cart on which they have dumped five hares and a fox, back legs tied together.

Early humans hunted of necessity for food, as remnant populations of hunter-gatherers do today, but it is no longer a necessity for the majority. Hunting endures, however, as an atavistic desire to see a creature flushed up into the sky or running helter-skelter across a field to be brought down, *crack–crack*, flailing out of the air on useless wings or bucking and jumping in a last paroxysm of nerves to lie still with its beautiful glazed eyes.

Not all men are like this. Most, on the surface, are not. But the urge is there, lurking in the mind, a violence turned outward on the natural world, and with monotonous regularity turned inward on ourselves, when we call it war. In the first twenty years of this century there have been wars in Afghanistan, Iraq,

Syria, Yemen, Libya, Congo, Nagorno-Karabakh, and most recently Ukraine. Millions of people have lost their lives or been displaced, whole cities obliterated, societies brought to such ruin they will take generations to recover. As it is now so it was in the twentieth and nineteenth centuries and as far back as there are records of the species. In the Middle Ages, my professor of medieval studies, Geoffrey Shepherd, used to say, peace was an interlude between wars. And when each war is over, through conquest or exhaustion, the victors are left as 'masters of the smoking ruins', as General Sir Edward Hamley wrote of the allies at Sebastopol at the end of the Crimean War.

This is something environmental campaigners never take into account when they project imagined solutions onto the great wave of natural disasters gathering to overwhelm us. It is a fatal flaw. We must start with what we are, and what we are reaches back to the way we evolved two hundred thousand years ago when anatomically modern humans first appear in the fossil record. Perhaps, even, we should go back 1.8 million years to the emergence of *Homo erectus*, the ancestor to *Homo ergaster*, humanity's own immediate forebear.

Advances in weaponry and the control of fire were key developments, leading to an increased diet of meat. This in turn enabled larger brains in relation to body weight to evolve, until today here we are, the last species of the genus and the most dominant and violent animal on Earth. Linnaeus indulgently named us *Homo sapiens* in his great classification of life, though *Homo destructor* would have been better, because however wise we are, or capable of being wise, the deep, dark side of our brain persists—Gellhorn with a gun.

Against Great Men

When Metternich, the Austrian foreign minister, met Napoleon in 1813, he taxed the Emperor with what he had done (as quoted in the *LRB*): 'In ordinary times armies are formed of only a small part of the population. Today it is the whole people that you have called to arms.' Metternich suggests that this is a disaster because so many of the very young died in the Russian campaign that it will affect future generations. Napoleon replied: 'You are no soldier and you do not know what goes on in the soul of a soldier. I was brought up in military camps, and a man such as I am does not give a fuck about the lives of a million men.' The reviewer calls this answer 'extraordinary' but it is not extraordinary at all. Napoleon was one of history's 'great men', and this is how great men think and how they behave.

Henry Fielding understood this when he wrote in the preface to *Jonathan Wild*, 'Greatness consists of bringing all manner of mischief on mankind, and Goodness in removing it… In the histories of Alexander and Caesar, we are frequently, and indeed impertinently, reminded of their benevolence and generosity, of their clemency and kindness. When the former had with fire and sword overrun a vast empire, had destroyed the lives of an immense number of innocent wretches, and had scattered ruin and desolation like a whirlwind,—we are told, as an example of his clemency, that he did not cut the throat of an old woman, and ravish her daughters, but was content with only undoing them.'

No one should be surprised by Napoleon's reply to Metternich, nor should anyone exalt him. He belongs in a grim gallery of portraits: Alexander, Caesar, Genghis Kahn, Tamburlaine, along with those who succeeded him, Stalin, Hitler, Mao Zedong, Pol Pot, Saddam Hussein, and more will come, great men who intoxicate the people, leading them to terrible acts of conquest, slaughter, destruction, pillage, rape, until the tide turns and the same horrors are inflicted on them in turn.

Make America Great Again, put the Great back in Great Britain. Trump and Johnson are Lilliputians standing on tiptoe on the steps leading to a rostrum where before long the next great man will appear.

The Elephant in the Room

The problem with schemes run up by environmentalists and governments to curb global warming is that they confuse an effect with its cause, in this case human overpopulation. In the last hundred years the human population has grown exponentially: 1930, 2 billion; 1960, 3 billion; 2020, 8 billion, finally levelling out, demographers think, at 9.8 billion in 2050. How many humans can the Earth sustain? Techno-optimists claim that genetic modification will produce a revolution in agriculture which will be able to feed 10 billion. But 10 billion people will need more than food. They will need housing, fresh water, energy, roads, railways, the infrastructure of complex industrialised societies. They will need more of the finite resources of the planet like rare earth metals. They will also need more land, as farmed land succumbs to desertification, as the demand for water for irrigation exhausts the aquifers, reduces the flow of rivers. New land will be seized by people who are desperate, or will be appropriated by agri-business, as is happening in the Brazilian rainforest.

But even if an agricultural revolution is achieved, there are likely to be billions left behind, as now, in poverty and below poverty. There is a finite supply of fresh water, and already too many in the world are without an adequate supply. Moreover, even if the last great forests of the Earth are felled, and the land farmed, it will only be a temporary solution. Cleared of its canopy of trees, the sparse earth of the great tropical forests is liable to serious erosion; the clearance, too, changes the climate, making it drier, destroying the sink for carbon, creating a positive feedback loop for global warming.

All this is without considering the pollution which 10 billion people will create. It is without considering the mass extinction of species which is already well under way, and which many biologists and ecologists think will reach the scale of the one 65 million years ago at the Cretaceous-Tertiary boundary, when something like 63 percent of all species then living became extinct. Some scientists argue that we need to prevent this on utilitarian grounds. There are still so many species that have not been described and named by science which may be a source for all kinds of drugs and other agents which might benefit humanity. This is no doubt true, but it does not seem to me the best argument for trying to halt this terrible process.

Most of us think of ourselves and ourselves alone. We are species-centric. But our genus, *Homo*, evolved over 2 million years, during most of which time we were only a part of something greater, the ever-changing self-renewing natural world. If we continue our destruction of the species with whom we share this world, we will destroy something in ourselves, will wound ourselves and carry the grief of it within us, even in the teeming megacities, whether we are aware of it or not.

Canute the Environmentalist

Recently, some scientists have proposed a new epoch for the period we live in—though this is not yet generally accepted—labelling it the Anthropocene, the Epoch of Man. For the first time in the 3.8-billion-year history of life, it is argued, one species has come to dominate the planet to such an extent that we have altered almost every aspect of it. Instead of being part of life on Earth, we have become the owners of it, and the promise of God in Genesis—'let them have dominion over the fish of the sea, and over the fowl of the air, and over the cattle, and over all the earth, and over every creeping thing that creepeth upon the earth'—has come to pass. Some well-meaning people argue that we should think of ourselves as the 'custodians' of other life on the planet—a kind of liberal interpretation of God's will in Genesis, but 'God' knew what he was doing, it is dominion that humans have always striven after, domesticating animals and plants that are useful to our survival, while eradicating everything that gets in our way.

Some would demur. What about the great national parks, organisations like the World Wide Fund for Nature dedicated to the preservation of the last wildernesses and the life they contain? They exist, it is true, but they haven't saved the Amazon rainforest or prevented species after species being added to the Red List. It is good that they exist and there have been successes—species brought back from the brink, wild places saved from loggers, mining corporations and other big exploiters. But it is one step forward, two steps back. Conservationists are engaged in a fighting retreat.

The Pattern in the Leaf

The sense of beauty in humans must derive from the natural world, within which we evolved—where else could it have come from? Beauty is concerned with balance and symmetry of the kind found in a butterfly's wings or the pattern of veins in a leaf. Art is not a copy of nature, not even the most 'realistic' or 'naturalistic' art, but an interpretation of it, a borrowing from it, a celebration of how we found ourselves where we are. Emil Nolde's flower paintings which are vivid splashes of colour, or Van Gogh's violent quivering portraits and landscapes are what they are, artefacts, but they make us see the world around us with a fresh intensity. Once you have looked at Nolde's *Grosser Mohn*, a seemingly hastily painted impression of large tousled red poppies, the painting superimposes itself on poppies in the external world, one interpreting the other, back and forth in the mind of the beholder.

It is tempting to say that a sense of beauty is innate in human beings, because it is something all cultures throughout history have admired and aspired toward in art. It is there in the great mosques of Islam, in the cathedrals of Europe, illustrated Celtic manuscripts, Chinese calligraphy, Japanese landscape paintings, the bark paintings of Australian Aborigines.

That this sense is derived from nature, and is even inherent in the laws of nature, is suggested by the beauty of aeroplanes like jet fighters and Concorde. Aeronautical designers and engineers did not set out to create something beautiful, they wanted the optimum design for supersonic flight. For this they had to understand the principles of aerodynamics and apply them to the machines they were designing. The result was a scaled-back purity of form which the eye perceives as beautiful. The mind can rebel against this. The purpose of a fighter is to deliver destruction and death (forget 'precision bombing'), while Concorde was a joint vanity product between Britain and France, flying across the Atlantic in a couple of hours at great environmental expense so the wealthy could conquer time. All the same, it is hard not to perceive them as beautiful forms in themselves. Some years ago, the Australian poet Les Murray told me he felt the same.

The problem of evil and beauty which the supersonic fighter encapsulates is hard to resolve. Totalitarian states like those of Stalin and Hitler rarely produce beauty. They present the iron mask of tyranny, reducing art to the utilitarian function of supporting and praising the regime. Those who refuse are denied access to publishing houses, galleries, concert halls, or they are imprisoned in gulags, exiled, even killed. So it was for Boris Pasternak and Victor Serge, for Kurt Weill and Thomas Mann.

But then there are artists who compromise in various degrees, who create great works of art in the interstices, as it were, of repression and terror, like Dmitri Shostakovich. And others, like Emil Nolde who was a Nazi sympathiser and remained so even after he fell foul of Hitler, when his art was condemned as 'degenerate' and he was forbidden to paint. How do we view his work, including the marvellous free-flowing watercolours of flowers that he produced in secret at his house in Seebüll after the prohibition? It would be easy to see them as tainted, and the righteous might say they should be destroyed. But when I visited Nolde's house, now a museum, on the German-Danish border, a room full of these 'illegal' paintings filled me with a sense of gladness and liberation which only great art can inspire. I reject Nolde's politics but I would not be without his paintings which are greater than the man.

So far as we know, only humans have a sense of beauty, though this may be the result of ignorance, of our inability to communicate with other species and so understand their perceptions of the world. If you believe in the truth of Iron Age creation myths like Genesis, the human sense of beauty is a gift from God. If you do not, then you have to say that beauty is a function of our brains, which are large in relation to body weight—large enough to respond to patterns in the universe which are innate in the functioning of matter, which are impersonal in themselves, but which the human mind delights in to such an extent that it plays with them in the art we create ourselves.

What Do We Really Feel About Nature?

Do humans have an innate affinity with the natural world? In 1984 the great entomologist and evolutionary biologist Edward O. Wilson published a book, *Biophilia*, subtitled *The Human Bond with Other Species*, in which he argued that this was indeed the case. It is an enticing proposition, and one which I would like to believe in. There is also superficial evidence for it in Western culture. We lavish great affection on dogs and cats, the animals we have domesticated as pets, and which give every sign that they respond to that affection. People surround themselves with other animals, too, from snakes and lizards, to budgerigars and lovebirds, and there is scarcely a house without pot plants of one kind or another. Carefully tended flower gardens are not as common as they were in my childhood, they nonetheless exist, and every city has its park where people like to stroll.

In 1993 Wilson followed up *Biophilia* with *The Biophilia Hypothesis*, a collection of essays co-edited with Stephen R. Gellert, in which leading biologists considered various aspects of his original idea. There was general agreement on the validity of the hypothesis, with one dissenting voice, that of Jared Diamond. Diamond had visited the New Guinea highlands periodically over thirty years, studying the birdlife, and living among the people. Highlanders had names for an impressive array of plants and animals which were of use to them economically, and revealed an intense interest in their natural surroundings, but they were less observant of species they had no use for. So the Foré, who Jared Diamond knew well, had only one word for 'butterfly' which served for all the species to be found in their territory.

Diamond also observed how Foré tribesmen treated the wild animals they captured. He describes what seems to us unspeakable cruelty—the breaking of a live animal's legs, for example, to make it easier for transport, and much worse. The Foré appeared to be indifferent to suffering. At other times they tortured captured animals for entertainment.

We might like to think we are different, but there are enough men who delight in badger-baiting and many more of us who turn a blind eye to the suffering of animals in the slaughterhouse before they appear as shrink-wrapped pieces of meat in the supermarket.

While I write, someone is shooting with a 12-bore on the outskirts of the village, killing crows and rooks, I suppose, because wildlife has dwindled to very little round here. The fields are all given over to grass for sheep. There are no grain crops, so the rooks and crows do no harm. But they are wild, and alive, and among the last creatures men can hunt for the joy of killing.

As I write, too, a small fly has become trapped in a spider's web strung across the outside of the windowpane. It struggles feebly, the vibrating strands of the web alerting the spider who runs swiftly from its hiding place, swaddles the fly, and carries it back alive to devour at leisure.

It cannot be said that nature is cruel. Nature simply *is*. But at life's inception some 3.8 billion years ago the adamantine rules were laid down. Every creature must eat to live, and every creature must breed. This applies to humans too, though thanks to our extraordinary brains, humans can make a choice which may be unique to our species. We can choose to break the circle. We can choose not to breed. The life force is strong, though, and few choose the even bleaker way of breaking the circle by killing themselves.

Biophilia exists in humans, in certain cultures at certain times, but biophobia exists too—a kind of war on the natural world which humans have fought for millennia, and which we still wage in spite of, or perhaps because of, our current temporary dominance.

A New Dark Age

We are living in a New Dark Age. How can this be? In a Dark Age, the physical infrastructure of a complex society collapses, leaving aftercomers to wonder at the ruins. One Anglo-Saxon poet, contemplating the ruins of an abandoned Roman fortress speculated that it must have been the work of giants. To think like this is to think of Dark Ages past, especially the collapse of the Roman Empire and the culture it sustained. What we have now is a different kind of collapse. We inhabit a world with a very sophisticated and ever-expanding superstructure, while our culture is exhausted and hollowed out.

There are many aspects to this and they may seem paradoxical. On the one hand, we have unprecedented access to knowledge through Wikipedia, through digital versions of our great libraries. Many archives, too, can be accessed online, and most magazines and journals have digital 'libraries' where you can consult back issues; films past and present are available online; there are virtual art galleries; hundreds of thousands of blogs, interviews, discussions, with some of the finest minds of the twentieth and twenty-first centuries. If you want a recipe—any recipe—you will find it online. Flower identification, birdsong identification, the fauna and flora of the Galapagos islands, what happened on Easter Island—it is all there. Moreover, thanks to Facebook, Twitter, Instagram, Skype, Zoom, we can communicate instantly with friends anywhere in the world; high-definition photographs can be snapped on iPhones; and there will be more and more as information technology expands its domain.

Such abundance should herald a Golden Age, but in fact it creates an overload of information as the mind flits from site to site grazing rather than patiently assimilating. One result is that memory becomes atrophied because you cannot process so much and such varied information, and in any case, you can always access it again via Google. We even have a verb for this, 'to google'.

This in turn affects our attention span. We no longer have time to read at leisure and at length. Newspaper articles rarely exceed 800 words and even once serious papers like *The Times* and *The Independent* have adopted a tabloid format with a dominance of image over text. A few serious cultural journals like *The London Review of Books*, *The New York Review of Books*, and in Wales *O'r Pedwar Gwynt* and *Planet*, still exist, but their readers are on the Red List of endangered species.

It can be argued that informed discussion of politics and cultural issues has moved to the Net. There is some truth to this. The problem is that serious engagement with these issues has to compete with millions of other voices all demanding to be heard at the same time, with everyone's opinion as good as everyone else's. It is an attitude which revels in ignorance under cover of a subversive populism, enabling demagogues like Trump and Johnson, ignorant themselves, to rise to political dominance.

The proliferation of 'social media' has played a large

role in this. During his four years in office in the White House, Trump almost governed by Twitter; campaigns of disinformation for political ends abound, whether homegrown or the work of foreign powers like Putin's Russia; websites of far-right groups foment class and race hatred. Public service broadcasters such as the BBC are under constant threat, accused of bias by successive Conservative and Labour governments. Powerful media owners like Rupert Murdoch and Tory newspapers like *The Daily Mail* run relentless campaigns of vilification against the Corporation and would like to destroy it. In America, Fox News dominates with its cynical distortions and lies, and if that is not far enough to the right, you can access alt-right online broadcasters like Breitbart News.

All of this feeds into a cynical postmodern attitude to truth—truth is relative, truth is what you say it is. There was a poor turn-out for Donald Trump's inauguration ceremony in 2017 but Trump insisted there were huge crowds and continued to do so despite filmed evidence to the contrary. 'Alternative facts' are very useful to politicians even when they are disbelieved by the majority, because they muddy the water, fomenting doubt or uncertainty, turning truth into a marketable commodity like everything else.

'"What is truth" said jesting Pilate, and would not stay for an answer.' But truth exists, as Bacon knew. It may be hard to come by; at times it may be impossible; but if we do not hold to truth as the bedrock of knowledge and experience, then we lose our hold on reality; we leave ourselves open to the lies and deceptions of those who would manipulate us.

Lying in Politics

The Washington Post has calculated that during his presidency Donald Trump told 20,000 lies up to July of this year. That makes him a Stakhanovite of lying and is very impressive. It would also be interesting to know how many times he told the truth. He must have now and then, if only by accident.

Trump has clearly been guided by the same principle as Napoleon who, according to his aide-de-camp, Philippe-Paul de Ségur, observed on the retreat from Moscow that 'In affairs of state one must never retreat, never retrace one's steps, never admit an error—that brings disrepute. When one makes a mistake, one must stick to it—that makes it right!'

This is no doubt an example of convergence common to the political mind. Trump said there was a large crowd at his inauguration, filmed evidence says there was not. The former President has, of course, long ago moved on from that particular 'error' and has told so many untruths since that he has probably forgotten about it, but he has not, so far as I know, retracted it.

This doesn't matter because Trump's lies are of a different order from those of Napoleon. Napoleon used lies advisedly. To be effective they had to be plausible, so that people believed them, or at least came to doubt the veracity of what was indeed the truth. Trump's lies are for the most part not crafted at all. They are on-the-hoof affairs, forgotten as soon as said. Their effect is of the moment and it doesn't matter if they are instantly exposed. He can get away with this because his followers don't care. They are under the spell of a myth—about the Deep State seizing control and destroying their freedoms. Only Trump can save freedom-loving America. He can lie as much as he likes, it is the slogans that count—*MAGA*, *Drain the Swamp*, *Lock Her Up*.

All politicians who gain high office become liars. There are many decent people in democratic politics, backbenchers who work hard for their constituents and who refuse to compromise their principles, but for those at the top the lying starts as soon as they are seated behind ministerial desks.

Where does that leave the mass of ordinary people, some of whom voted them into power, all of whom are ruled by them until the next general election? It seems to me that even if you voted for the incumbents, you must switch at once to become part of the 'opposition'. By this I mean that you should stand back and sift what any government says, to discover what it is *really* saying, and respond accordingly. 'Truth kills everybody,' Ted Hughes wrote in *Crow*, but lies kill too, and political lies, unchallenged, kill democracy.

The Attraction of War

For the past several years I have been reading about British wars in the nineteenth century—not historical studies of them, but first-hand accounts by participants or by eyewitnesses. So I read G.R. Gleig's *The Subaltern* and *A Narrative of the Campaigns of the British Army at Washington and New Orleans*, Philippe-Paul de Ségur's *Defeat: Napoleon's Russian Campaign*, Lady Sale's *A Journal of the Disasters in Afghanistan, 1841-2*, Major Ashe's *Personal Records of the Kandahar Campaign*, and A.W. Kinglake's 9-volume *The Invasion of the Crimea*. A book by an historian would have provided a nuanced interpretation of these campaigns, but what I wanted was the *immediacy*, the sense of *being there*, which first-hand accounts provide, no matter how self-serving or inaccurate they inevitably are at times. Moreover, wherever possible I bought and read them in first editions, or near-first editions, because the feel of the paper, the print, the sometimes beautifully tooled leather bindings, the bookplates or signatures of previous owners, took me *physically* closer to those times.

Growing up in the shadow of the First and Second World Wars (two uncles fought in the First, four cousins in the Second, one uncle badly wounded, one cousin killed, two badly wounded) I had a belief that in earlier centuries war could not have been as bad, because armies lacked the destructive potential of modern weaponry. I was wrong.

Nineteenth-century artillery may have consisted of muzzle-loading canons, but solid cannonballs, grapeshot, exploding shells, could wreak fearful damage. De Ségur recounts how one Russian cannonball killed twenty men who were assembled side-on to the line of fire; when Napoleon inspected the field after one battle, the dead and dying were so thickly strewed about that his horse and those of his entourage couldn't avoid stepping on them. He began the Russian campaign with 450,000 men. Five months later, some 20,000 survived the terrible winter retreat. (Napoleon, the madman, had detached himself from the remnants to rush back to Paris with the aim of raising another army of 350,000.)

In *The Subaltern*, Gleig describes what happened when Wellington's army finally broke into the besieged city of St Sebastian—for two days the British troops were out of their officers' control, looting, killing, raping, lying dead drunk in the streets, only to start all over again the following day. The same happened in Russia—villages, towns, cities burned to the ground; crops and forage seized for miles around, leaving the people who weren't killed destitute and starving; the wagon train piled ever higher with loot. In *The Subaltern*, Gleig goes to inspect the field of battle after a British cavalry charge. He comes across one French soldier with his head cleaved down to his eyes, another with his face split open like a melon, the sabre being a deadly weapon, cavalry a deadly force.

My generation has been exceptionally lucky in that it has not had to fight. I missed National Service by eighteen months. Korea, the colonial wars in Malaya, Kenya, and elsewhere, were fought by the luckless generation slightly older than me. I suppose that had I been called up I would have gone. I doubt I would have had the courage to be a conscientious objector, and perhaps I did not have the attitude to war I have now. Born in 1941, my early childhood was lived at the edge of the Second World War—lines of sand-coloured army vehicles passing our house, my father's rifle too heavy to lift. I played with Dinky Toy Spitfires and Flying Fortresses, and had a rather good collection of Army vehicles of the period—field artillery, ammunition trucks, tanks, lorries, jeeps. In the 1950s I watched films—*The Dambusters* and many others glorifying Britain's role in the war against Nazi Germany. When I see them now, I do so with different eyes—see the propaganda in them, the way horror, hurt, and suffering, are airbrushed out.

But war still attracts—for each generation remembers nothing, or too little, of the past. When the fleet sailed from Portsmouth in 1982 to recover the Falklands, military bands played, women and children crowded the harbour walls cheering and waving Union Jacks, the aircraft carrier was accompanied by countless small boats bobbing at its sides and in its wake. It was a grand adventure, something to be proud of—with the horror to come, as it had been again and again in the nineteenth century.

The Problem of Religion

I have always had a problem with religion, never having believed even with the naiveté of a child. It was forced on me however in my schools and by compulsory attendance at church on Sundays, for which, in a way, I am grateful. It gave me a good grounding in certain key books of the Bible which I have reinforced by reading Genesis, the Gospels, the Revelation of St John the Divine, several times since. Readings from the Bible in school assemblies and at church services also gave me my first introduction to poetry, although I didn't know this at the time. I am referring of course to the King James Bible, the only version worth reading if you are a speaker of English.

In every other way I find religion—any religion—an affront. Religion breeds sectarianism and righteous violence against those who believe otherwise. Catholics versus Protestants, Sunnis versus Shias, Muslims versus Hindus—millions have died in wars caused by absolutist faith which makes men and women righteous and cruel.

Millions more have had their cultures destroyed by missionary zeal—by the arrogance of Christian missionaries, especially, who spread across early medieval Europe destroying or appropriating Pagan religious sites and beliefs, and doing the same centuries later in the Americas and Africa. (Sometimes they got their comeuppance—Boniface was murdered in Frisia in 754 AD after cutting down a sacred oak. He was, of course, made into a Martyr and a Saint, dying for the faith being a speciality of the early Christians.)

There is a more fundamental objection to religion, however, which is that all religions superimpose a pattern of meaning on the universe which makes sense of our place in it—if you believe, that is. Even during the thousand-year dominance of the Ptolemaic system it was clear that the universe was vast, and that life on Earth for most people was brutal and short, which, Genesis explains, was a consequence of God's curse on Adam at the time of the Fall: 'cursed is the ground for thy sake; in sorrow shalt thou eat of it all the days of thy life; Thorns also and thistles shall bring it forth to thee; and thou shalt eat the herb of the field; In the sweat of thy face shalt thou eat bread, till thou return unto the ground; for out of it thou wast taken: for dust thou art, and unto dust shalt thou return.'

But then there was the coming of Jesus Christ when the God of Anger and Revenge transmuted into the God of Love, holding out hope of salvation—not here, not now, but in the blue beyond, provided, that is, we live by His precepts, the obverse of salvation being eternal damnation, so meticulously chronicled by Dante and Hieronymus Bosch, and in the crude murals in parish churches throughout the European Middle Ages. Times change, and Christianity changes with them. Many denominations prefer to avoid Hell and damnation these days, emphasising instead the God of Love and Forgiveness. Indeed, a friend of mine from Abergavenny days who became Bishop of Winnipeg, preached that the God of Mercy would save everybody in the end. A win-win scenario.

In the interstices, as it were, of intolerance and periodic violence, religions are capable of doing many good things—giving succour to the homeless, comforting the dying and the bereaved, providing a sense of community and hope, and above all offering an all-enfolding vision of the universe and a meaningful place in it for frail, questing humanity.

This is true, but it is also delusional. I don't mean the urge to provide help and comfort to those who need it—most of us need it most of the time. I mean the worldview, the vision of humanity's place in the universe, and the stories religions tell to illuminate this—because there is a serpent in the Garden of Faith—science.

Since the beginning of the nineteenth century advances in geology, evolutionary biology, palaeoanthropology, physics, astronomy, cosmology, have cast powerful beams of light on the material universe. The Ptolemaic system placed Man and the Earth at the centre; the Copernican system made it heliocentric; modern astronomy displaces everything—we are the inhabitants of a planet circling a medium-sized star on one wing of a spiral galaxy among billions of galaxies containing billions of stars. Moreover, the Earth was not created in 4004 BC, as Archbishop Ussher calculated in the seventeenth century—it is some 4.6 billion years old; nor was our species, *Homo sapiens*, created on the sixth day according to Genesis; rather, we evolved over two million years from a remote ancestor species, *Homo habilis*, via *Homo erectus* and

Homo ergaster. At one time we modern humans shared the Earth with other human species, notably *Homo erectus*, and famously, the Neanderthals.

All of this is well documented and beyond dispute, and it undermines religious interpretations of the world which humans have believed in for millennia. 'Human kind / Cannot bear very much reality,' wrote T.S. Eliot, who, being a High Anglican, could not bear very much reality himself. Nevertheless, many millions prefer to deny the evidence of science, or try to match up the evidence with the teachings of religion. Jehovah's Witnesses who come to the door explain that when it says in Genesis that the Earth and all things in it were created in six days, a 'day' here means 'a very long time', so science merely fleshes out what the Bible says. They are silent on human evolution, though.

There are as many who deny science altogether, who prefer to live in a make-believe world. A recent poll suggests that 77 percent of Americans believe in angels. Even in secular, materialistic Britain 33 percent of the population are said to do so according to one survey. And then of course there is Islam.

In the West there appear to be two opposing trends—one in the direction of materialism and a 'whatever' shrug towards religion; the other falling back on an intensification and hardening of religious attitudes, especially in America. Neither is much interested in truth as revealed by science, though each uses the inventions of science and technology such as the Web to promote their preference, whether to persuade us to 'consume' ever more of capitalism's products, or to lure us by the full-on appeal of internet evangelism.

Religion, it is clear, will never die. It has too powerful a hold on the needs of too many human beings. 'Live and let live' is a good rule of thumb for a democratic society—let a thousand delusions blossom. Religion becomes a threat, though, when it is yoked to State power, and especially when it *becomes* the State, as in a theocracy. A few hundred years ago, the views expressed here would have had me burned at the stake in Europe. Even today, in many parts of the world, you would be whipped, stoned, or beheaded, for expressing them.

Poetry on Trial

In the summer, *Poetry*, the magazine founded by Harriet Monroe in 1912, published a poem, 'Scholl's Ferry Rd.' by Michael Dickman. It is not a very long poem, but it spreads over thirty pages, including four pages at the end with only one line apiece. Blank space is used imaginatively here to suggest the increasingly blank spaces in an old lady's life as she succumbs to dementia. The poem is narrated by a grandchild who partly observes her decline, and partly reports on the old lady's jumble of memories, her irascibility at times with family members, her struggle against inevitable defeat. It is rather a good poem, but it caused a huge fuss in the American poetry world because of two passages which traumatised a number of readers, so they claimed, because of its deep-dyed racism.

The reaction of the Editor and of The Poetry Foundation, the wealthy organisation which publishes *Poetry*, was swift and extreme. The print copy of the issue was withdrawn from circulation and pulped, the poem was deleted from the magazine's website, and the Editor, Don Share, resigned. It is impossible to find 'Scholls Ferry Rd.' anywhere—at least, I was unable to locate it until an acquaintance loaned me a copy of the print edition which had escaped the bonfire. It must be a rarity now.

Here is the passage which caused most offense:

'Negress' was another word she liked to use

That's the nice way to say it

'Oh they are always changing what they want to be called'

On the bus she dropped her purse
I was with her
A nice Negress handed it back

She put out her hand to receive it the whole time looking out
the window never said a word

Hours later
'What a nice Hawaiian'

This scene, set perhaps in the '60s, is a carefully nuanced account of the racial attitudes of a white woman who has, certainly, a prejudice against black people but who wants to appear to do the right thing, say the right thing, when the woman hands her the purse. She knows or thinks she knows that 'Negro/Negress' is the accepted term for African-Americans, which it was at one time, yet she looks out of the bus window as the woman passes over the purse—she looks away—and later says 'What a nice Hawaiian', which might reflect the confused mind of the dementia sufferer, or might be a deflection from the truth of the incident—or it might be both.

What happened is part of the poem, it is not the attitude of the poet, and is certainly not intended as an incitement to racial hatred. It is a reflection of the truth of the genteel attitudes of a certain class of white woman at a certain point in history. There can be no mistake about this, and yet it caused such outrage that The Poetry Foundation pulped the issue.

According to Jay Sizemore, who wrote a very good online response to the affair—'How Cancel Culture Has Ruined Literary Criticism'—the scandal started when one Hana Shapiro tweeted: 'It's pretty unacceptable that you would publish this, especially during a time when so many POC [People of Colour] are grieving/being targeted. Shouldn't you be focusing on amplifying Black voices right now?' This was picked up and rapidly became a 'Twitter-storm' repeated, I am sure, by many who had never read the poem, just as many of the faithful who bayed for Salman Rushdie's death had never seen a copy of *The Satanic Verses*, let alone read it.

No matter, the protest worked, and the Editor, Don Share, wrote an abject farewell apology in which he 'accepts sole responsibility for publishing the poem' and 'apologize[s] unreservedly for doing so'. The poem 'egregiously voices offensive language that is neither specifically identified nor explicitly condemned as racist. It also centres completely on white voices, leaving room for no other presences.' '...I failed to understand that the poem I thought I was reading was not the one that people would actually read'. He writes of his 'poor judgement', he resigns 'with the deepest regret that I brought hurtful language to these pages, words which had a terrible impact. I failed to live up to my own values, but much worse and more significantly, failed readers who came to our pages in good faith and the hopefulness that poetry promises.'

Such abjectness is dispiriting. Don Share capitulated at once. He was 'wrong', he confesses—but 'wrong' in the face of aggressive group-think which prefers outraged anger to careful consideration of what the poem is about. It is a form of bullying to which white liberals are particularly sensitive, which places them on the defensive because of their position as whites.

Don Share was right to publish 'Scholls Ferry Rd.'. His initial sense of the poem's worth was correct and should have been defended. Instead, a Twitter storm by the righteous brought him down. His farewell 'Editor's Note' has echoes, if faint ones, of the Moscow show trials where 'confession' was a formality—the verdict, 'guilty', already known. Presumably, Don Share was not taken to the basement of The Poetry Foundation and shot in the back of the neck, but he confessed in a show trial by the 'right-on' and symbolically, at least, suffered the same fate.

31/10/2020

Contempt for Truth

There is a distrust of experts, of people with specialised knowledge. This is encouraged by populist newspapers and the 'blogosphere'. It's the people who count and anyone's opinion is as good as anyone else's. This attitude has opened the door to a wide range of conspiracy theories, and 'alternative' truths. The Covid-19 pandemic doesn't exist, or if it does it was manufactured and deliberately released by the Chinese. Vaccines are dangerous, an attempt by the government at mind-control of the populace. G-5 masts are the cause of the virus, or the cause of whatever alternative plot is touted on Facebook and Twitter. Experts can patiently explain the facts as they are known, but experts are elitists.

This is either self-deceiving or dishonest because a complex society is criss-crossed with elites and we would not survive long without them. If your house needs rewiring, you find a qualified electrician. For heart surgery, you turn to a surgeon, not someone off the street armed with *Gray's Anatomy* and a scalpel.

The contempt for expertise tends to concentrate on areas where an element of uncertainty is implicit in the data so it becomes easier to dispute expert opinion. Science is vulnerable to this kind of assault. Evolutionary biology, for example, is itself constantly evolving with subsets of hypotheses proposed to explain phenomena that seem to be anomalous. This is particularly true in a rapidly changing field like palaeoanthropology where almost every new fossil discovery has the potential to change the clade of our genus *Homo*. Is *Homo ergaster* a distinct species or a European variant of *Homo erectus*? Is the recently discovered *Homo floresiensis* a true species, a diminutive member of *Homo erectus*, or *Homo sapiens*, suffering perhaps from island dwarfism?

There is, however, universal agreement among biologists that species evolve through natural selection and that human beings are no exception. The evidence for this is detailed and overwhelming. Christian fundamentalists nonetheless deny it. The most naïve ones simply fall back on biblical authority—the Earth and everything in it was created in six days. Genesis is the Word of God. The science is wrong. The more sophisticated realise that this is not enough to convince anyone who has sipped the 'poison' of science, inventing in its place the pseudo-science of Creationism which mimics the procedures of science and has the appearance of intellectual rigour but it is based on a demonstrably false premise. It has powerful advocates in the USA, however, who lobby for it to be taught in schools and colleges as a valid 'alternative' to evolutionary biology. This is a case of experts in a field being challenged by pseudo-experts who attract large numbers of the willing and gullible to their cause. Suddenly 'experts' are acceptable.

History offers even greater scope for falsification because, by its very nature, it is provisional. Even where facts are established, each generation interprets them in its own way, history acting as a reflection of the present as much as the past. Because of this, history books eventually become a part of history themselves. The subjectivity inherent in the study of the past has its limits, however. Documentary evidence for the Holocaust is overwhelming and is taken into account by every serious historian of Nazi Germany. Holocaust-deniers, like historian David Irving, distort or suppress evidence to make the case that it never happened. Irving is a pseudo-expert and his counter-history has been comprehensively disproved and discredited.

A more recent example is the use of history by right-wing proponents of Brexit who argue that Britain is still a world power capable of 'punching above its weight' once it has freed itself from the EU. The argument draws on a powerful British myth about the Second World War, in which 'plucky' Britain stood alone against Nazi Germany in 1940 and—in its most extreme version—went on to win, with a little help from the Empire and the Americans. The fact that it was Russia who turned the tide against Hitler at huge cost to itself, and that Britain could not have held out without massive material support from America, and that the Normandy invasion could not have taken place without American troops, is swept into a dusty corner of history.

Then there is the fact, too, that Britain's 'greatness' was dependent on its worldwide empire; that this was beginning to unravel in India and elsewhere even before the war; and that it collapsed spectacularly in the post-war years, leaving Britain a prosperous but middle-ranking power on the fringes of the European continent. During the referendum campaign of 2016 truth was replaced by myth and we will have to live with the consequences for many years to come. Britain will not rise like a giant freed from its shackles. It will struggle to find its imagined place in the world. Economically and politically it will become ever more dependent on America, itself an empire that contains the seeds of its own destruction.

All of this is clear if you study the history of the past seventy years. In 2016, however, too many preferred the pseudo-history of demagogues like Boris Johnson and Nigel Farage because it fed into their sense of outrage; because it made them feel good.

Would-Be Dictators

Donald Trump never reached the status of dictator, though he had the dictator's mentality and ambition and was capable of inspiring his followers with unthinking devotion tinged with an aura of violence. During his four years as president, America's perception of itself as the world's leader in democratic values was severely strained, and it remains to be seen whether Joe Biden can rebalance the political and judicial systems on which democracy depends.

Trump was a fantasist who persuaded millions that his fantasies were real. How far he believed them himself is difficult to say, or indeed whether he believed in anything except the dream of himself as the great leader. Now he has fallen, though he will never admit that he lost in a democratic election. He will always have been cheated; the election snatched from him by the forces of darkness, the Deep State, the swamp he so heroically tried to drain.

Unlike real dictators, Trump was a comic would-be one. At the end, Hitler shot himself through the mouth in the labyrinth of chambers beneath the Chancellery. Mussolini was shot by a partisan and hung upside down from a girder. Gaddafi was found hiding in a drainpipe and shot. Trump retires to his golf course and grainy telephoto-lens footage shows him teeing off.

What will he do now? He was pumped up by his own ego, he was Mussolini-like in his huge delight in the adoration of crowds of MAGA baseball-cap-wearing supporters, but the illusion of the mighty figure towering and swaying above reality has been deflated and brought to ground. Perhaps he will go back to a new series of *The Apprentice* where he can swagger and preen and preside in judgement over young men and women desperate to be as rich, brash and vulgar as himself. Perhaps he will build more golf courses, more condominiums, surround himself with gold. Or perhaps he will be prosecuted for his many misdemeanours which couldn't happen while he was in office.

Meanwhile, we had Boris Johnson with his lurching parody of Churchill's famous brow-down gait— making Britain great again, leading his people in a reprise of their finest hour. But he is not a Churchillian bulldog, he is a stuffed toy replica, and already the stuffing is coming out. Despite this, or because of it, he has done damage to the democratic system, purging his party of its liberal wing, seeking to evade parliamentary scrutiny, indulging in blatant cronyism. Johnson is Trump-lite, a parody of a parody. Now that he has been ousted by a palace coup, where will he turn? Back to writing blustering lying columns for the *Telegraph*? He will certainly be offered lucrative directorships, be in demand for well-paid lecture tours and after-dinner speeches. He will not be desperately scrabbling around for a minimum-wage zero-hour-contract job or standing in line at a food bank, as many will when the economic crisis caused by the pandemic is deepened by our discovery of the true price of Brexit.

Revolution's Allure

Humanity is haunted by the dream of perfection. When it is imagined in the future we call it utopia. When it is located in the past it is the golden age. The first golden age was the Garden of Eden, but we were cast out of that by man's sin and have been seeking its entrance ever since.

The first great revolution of modern times, the French, promised a new paradise, though before it could be achieved the corrupt old order had to be destroyed. The guillotine did fine work slicing off heads. Once blood flows, however, it is difficult to stop. The Revolution led to the Terror, and the Terror to Napoleon, to European conquest and slaughter and the catastrophe of the invasion of Russia. Hundreds upon hundreds of thousands of people died, lands were laid waste.

But the dream continued. Barely a hundred years later, the Bolshevik revolution of 1917 declared a paradise for the people. Class distinctions were to be abolished; the aristocracy and the bourgeoisie stripped of their wealth; their estates redistributed to the peasants; the proletariat were to govern industry themselves. People had to die for this to be achieved, not by the guillotine now, but shot in the back of the neck in prison cellars, because from the beginning there were weeds in the garden who had to be rooted out, and a police force equal to the job—the Cheka, GPU, OGPU, GUGB, NKGB, NKVD, KGB, acronyms as ugly as their deeds.

The utopia of the Bolsheviks collapsed as quickly as that of the French, and those naïve enough to believe in its possibility were among the first to be rounded up in the gulag, to be interrogated, admitting to imaginary crimes, to counter-revolutionary activities, so their execution could be justified by the mockery of their own false confessions. Some even did so gladly, believing their sacrifice to be necessary for the glory of the revolutionary future.

Joseph Conrad understood this with clear penetration. In *Under Western Eyes* published in 1911, the English narrator observes to Nathalie Haldin: '... in a real revolution—not a simple dynastic change or a mere reform of institutions—in a real revolution the best characters do not come to the front. A violent revolution falls into the hands of narrow-minded fanatics and of tyrannical hypocrites at first. Afterwards comes the turn of the pretentious intellectual failures of the time. Such are the chiefs and leaders. You will notice that I have left out the mere rogues. The scrupulous and the just, the noble, human, and devoted natures; the unselfish and the intelligent may begin a movement—but it passes away from them. They are not the leaders of a revolution. They are its victims: the victims of disgust, of disenchantment—often of remorse. Hopes grotesquely betrayed, ideals caricatured—that is the definition of revolutionary success.' What Conrad foresaw so clearly was witnessed at first hand by Victor Serge, and documented in novels like *Conquered City* and *Midnight in the Century*, and in his *Memoirs of a Revolutionary*.

For the time being revolution is out of fashion, the revolutionary spirit exhausted. The trend now is toward dictatorship allied with greed. Grab what you can. If you do not, you are a fool, or one of the weak. Not everyone thinks like this. There are many who lead decent lives, who are concerned about what is happening to democracy and to the Earth, but the governing ethos is not in their favour. Look at Trump, Bolsonaro, Erdogan, Putin, Assad, Modi, Johnson. Trump, it is true, has gone, but his followers have not—nearly half of those who voted in the 2020 election voted for him, and he is likely to remain a force in American politics, raging on the outside, the spoiler destabilising any attempt to return to decent democratic values.

The truth is an open book for all to read—human nature, as it has evolved in our genus for 1.8 million years, is imperfect, our brains jury-rigged, our lives governed by irrational swings, so that what we build we eventually destroy. And the natural world, out of which we evolved, is like this, too—forever in flux, beautiful and terrible at the same time. Nothing is stable, and utopia assumes stability, an equilibrium in which humanity will at last achieve a brilliant apotheosis. It cannot be. At least myths of golden ages past contained within their stories the seeds of their own destruction. The great revolutions of the past two hundred years were always flawed beyond help, for in every Paradise a serpent lurks.

Weepy Culture

The BBC4 series *The Repair Shop* begins with the conceit of a beautiful thatched barn-like structure set in an idyllic rural landscape. It is always summer or early autumn. It is peaceful and usually the sun is shining. In this barn—the repair shop—a group of craftspeople are busy at their benches. There is a leather-worker, a picture restorer, wood- and metalworkers, a specialist in all things mechanical. There is an atmosphere of quiet busyness and co-operation—the woodworker may be restoring a chair but goes to the leatherworker to reupholster the seat. Every tool, machine, paint, glue, wood, metal, fabric, you can imagine is there.

Each week, four members of the public bring along some treasured family possession which needs repairing. Usually it is the only thing they have by which to remember a deceased mother/father/grandmother/grandfather. The participants are usually old or late middle aged themselves, and the majority are English. They are greeted by the relevant expert, tell their story, exit the barn, and leave the specialist to get on with the job of repairing.

Now the interesting part of the programme begins, as the craftsmen and women get to work—the delicacy, the skill, the ingenuity, the infinite variety of tools are fascinating to watch, and of course each heirloom is restored to perfection. Then the owner returns (or owners, because sometimes it is a husband and wife, or grandmother and grandson). The object is under a cover. 'Do you want to see it?' 'Oh I can't wait!' and the cover is slowly withdrawn to reveal the miracle wrought by the repair team.

There follows what seems to me a very strange reaction. The owner, especially if it is a woman, looks in amazement. Often she raises both hands to her cheeks in that visual signal for shock or intense surprise. Perhaps she (or he) says 'Oh my goodness!!' and tears well up and the owner has to turn away. There is pitying sympathy in the gaze of the craftsperson, followed, if the owner is a woman, by hugs and back-pattings. 'Oh, I can't thank you enough! Grandma/Grandpa/Mum/ Dad [delete as applicable] will be looking down now so pleased! Thank you! Thank you!' 'You're welcome!' and the person walks out of the workshop clutching the prized object for a final statement to camera where he or she repeats her gratitude, sometimes again with tears.

The programme seems strange to me because it combines two very different things—fascination with the practical skill of the craftspeople who live in a world of wood shavings, soldering, specialist glues, drills, fretsaws, hard-earned knowledge—and a teary, blurry world that seems contrived, with sentiment blown up into sentimentality that is embarrassing to watch.

All such programmes are carefully choreographed of course, and we never hear the director's instructions to the owners, never see the false starts and repeats. The show is seamlessly edited and tailored to appeal to what is virtually a pandemic of sentimentality at the moment.

The first time I noticed this tendency was in the aftermath of the death of Princess Diana in 1997, when millions mourned the passing of a woman who in between patronising good causes—which all royals are expected to do—spent unimaginable wealth on designer dresses, jewellery, upmarket restaurants, exotic holidays, while conducting a very public feud with her husband. What were they weeping for? Hardly anyone who cried openly had come anywhere near Diana, yet to them she was an icon, a saint almost, of a materialist world that is all surface. They were weeping buckets perhaps for themselves, because death had smashed the mirror and there was nothing behind it.

The earliest example of weepiness of which I am aware, is Chaucer's description of the Prioress in the Prologue to *The Canterbury Tales*:

> She was so charitable and so pitous
> She wolde wepe, if that she saugh a mous
> Kaught in a trappe, if it were deed or bledde.
> Of smale houndes had she that she fedde
> With rosted flesh, or milk and wastel-breed.
> But soore wept she if oon of hem were deed,
> Or if men smoot it with a yerde smerte;
> And al was conscience and tendre herte.

The Prioress is in a way an amalgam of Princess Diana and the weepy crowd. As a nun she ought not to keep lapdogs, or imitate the manners of the royal court, as she does, or bedeck herself with jewellery ('Of small coral about hire arm she bar / A peire of bedes, gauded al with grene, / And thereon heng a brooch of gold ful sheene / On which ther was first write a crowned A / And after *Amor vincit omnia*.') *Amor vincit omnia* (Love conquers all) is a nice touch. Is it love of God or love of the World? Like Diana, the Prioress tries to have it both ways, demur and devout but also something of a fourteenth-century fashion plate, addicted to material possessions.

The interesting thing here is that, while Chaucer clearly has a soft spot for this delicate transgressor of her Order's rules, at the same time he sends her up with the gentlest of satires, for every word in his description of her is ironic and must be read two ways.

The Prioress is the only character I can think of in Chaucer's vast oeuvre, or indeed in Middle English literature, who weeps in a sentimental way at the drop of a hat, and she is clearly not presented as someone to emulate. There are no doubt other examples in the literature of later centuries, but I cannot think of any before the fashion for 'sensibility' in the late eighteenth century, epitomised by Henry Mackenzie's novel *The Man of Feeling* (1771) which was immensely popular for a time. In the Victorian period, too, a weepy sentimentality was prevalent, as a dip into any novel by Dickens can confirm.

I think the current vogue derives, in part at least, from America. When I first encountered Americans in the early '60s I was extremely surprised, and slightly embarrassed, by the way they treated you as their very best friend, even though you had only met them once or twice. I was equally surprised by the way individuals who I *did* think of as friends discarded you as soon as they returned to the States. American expression of feeling seemed (and still seems) exaggerated beyond the demands of the moment and therefore inherently insincere. Many aspects of American culture end up being imitated in Britain, and the fashion for gushing, weepy sentiment seems to be among them.

But then there is television and social media like Facebook which facilitate real-time images and sound, making it very easy to expose your feelings publicly. Now on TV news channels, hardly an evening goes by without someone on a sofa parading their grief, wiping away tears, or breaking off—'I'm sorry...'—overcome with emotion, while we, the viewers, sit on our sofas with a coffee, watching. It is so ubiquitous that for the most part we don't think how strange, how voyeuristic it is. Nor, it seems, do the people exposing a grief that should be private, that should not be broadcast mawkishly into millions of homes.

Nothing can be done about it for the time being. It is deeply engrained in mass culture that weeping copiously in public is not only alright, it is expected, with the implication that there is something wrong with you if you hold back or disapprove.

It would be interesting to go behind the scenes at *The Repair Shop*. Are participants coaxed by the director? How many takes are made of the unveiling scene until they get just the right amount of excess emotion? Most candidates, of course, will be familiar with the programme's format beforehand and so will know what is expected of them, and will do their best to live up to it, unlike the Scot in this week's episode who said the experts had done a good job, shook hands warmly, and left without a tear in sight.

Religion of Blood and Delusion

I don't understand the religious mind, no doubt because I have never been religious. The universe is a rational place, otherwise organised matter could not exist. Aha! the religionist will say, that means there has to be a rational mind that created it! But this is Paley's watch all over again. Because the human mind has evolved so that it can perceive order in matter, it does not necessarily imply that that order was created by a rational mind, something like ours, no doubt, but far mightier.

We will probably never be able to see beyond the event horizon of the big bang some 13.8 billion years ago, so there will be a mystery forever at the heart of our knowledge. This of course gives licence for belief in a Prime Mover who set the universe in motion. On this premise religionists have built a superstructure of apparent reason. It is, however, like the house built on sand—its foundations are weak and eventually it collapses. Instead of shifting to build on a solid foundation, however, religionists rebuild on sand again and again, for all that can truly be said about the moment before the big bang is that *we know nothing about it*.

When you look closely at a religion like Christianity, you see that it is deeply irrational and cobbled together from a mishmash of myths, legends, history, and unsubstantiated 'miracles', going far beyond what the rational mind can accept. Walking on water? Raising the dead? Transforming a few loaves and fishes to feed a multitude? Rising from the dead oneself after a terrible execution? The mind rebels. These are primitive beliefs arising from a primitive mindset, no matter how many subtle arguments theologians adduce in support of them.

And there is more. Seen from outside, Christianity is a strange and barbaric system of belief. God sends his 'only begotten Son' to Earth to bring salvation to humanity, to save them from Sin—the Sin of course being the result of the Fall and the expulsion from Eden, a scenario set up by God in the first place. Leaving aside the malice of a god who punishes later generations for the sin of the first humans, the life of the Son on Earth is abhorrent, particularly when he makes that fateful journey to Jerusalem, believing he must be sacrificed so humanity can be saved.

There follows the public whipping, the humiliation, the pain, the jeering of the mob, the nails driven into hands and feet, the raising of the Cross, the long agonising hours hanging there. What kind of God are we being asked to believe in who would stand by and allow this to happen because sinful Man must be 'saved'? He is a puppet-master, pulling the strings of live puppets who are jerked across the stage of this contrived drama.

And what comes after the suffering? The magic of the empty tomb followed by the Ascension. This is the Rock Peter built on, a rock smeared with blood and gore. The religious are reminded of this every time they kneel at the altar-rail for holy communion, receiving the wafer and the wine at the hands of the priest. It matters little whether, like Roman Catholics, you believe this to be the body and blood of Jesus Christ, miraculously transubstantiated, or whether, like Anglicans, you believe they are symbolic. What you are being asked to do is engage in a form of ersatz cannibalism—eating the flesh and drinking the blood of your God.

Christianity is a religion of blood, the blood of the Lamb, the blood of the Martyrs; blood to the end of a bloody world (cf The Book of Revelation)—but a world which *in fact* is material and rational. Animal life is rational. Watching film of a lion claw down a gazelle and proceed to eat it alive is horrible, but it is eminently rational in terms of the way life on Earth has evolved over some 3.8 billion years. What is not rational is humanity with our jury-rigged brain, our brutality against our own kind, the adherence of many to religious primitivism which throughout history has been the cause of violent intolerance. We would be far better off without it but that is unlikely ever to happen.

Centres and Peripheries

It is natural to think in terms of centres and peripheries. A capital city has everything, government, banking, embassies, publishing houses, national museums, theatres, concert halls, opera houses, and more and more. Anyone with ambition gravitates there. Ancillary 'centres' may exist like Oxford and Cambridge, but they act as feeders for the real centre, in this case London. Beyond the centre, by definition, is the periphery, which goes by various derogatory names—backwoods, backwaters—where yokels live. Part of this periphery of course is the 'Celtic fringe' inhabited by paddies, taffies and jocks.

If you live on the edge you feel the centripetal pull. In these islands, for centuries, if you wanted to make a name for yourself you had to make it in London. And it is still true, because on the periphery you are always facing the centre, while the centre most definitely will not be facing you.

You may wish to challenge this and turn away, but there is a cruel ironical fact—to gain recognition as an artist, musician, composer, dramatist, poet, novelist, you have to gain recognition at the centre. The attention you attract there will be reflected back to where you happen to be, because the periphery deals in reflected light, just as the Moon reflects the light of the Sun.

This has been especially true for English-language writers in Wales—even for so thoroughgoing a patriot as R.S. Thomas. He published almost all his books with

London publishers, or in later years, with Bloodaxe, a leading provincial English publisher. His subject was Wales (and God), but as far as his publishing career was concerned, his gaze was fixed on England.

Publishers in Wales can rarely keep their most successful authors, for, like it or not, they act as nurseries for the far bigger London publishers, and Welsh authors almost to a man or woman leap at the chance of being published there. The rest are small fry not worth the catch.

Coming from the 'Celtic fringe' myself—and indeed from a fringe of the fringe in the border town of Abergavenny—I had these attitudes myself, and for many years I tried to get published in English magazines and submitted poetry collections to London publishers without success. What Australians call the 'cultural cringe' *vis-à-vis* London is powerful, and I cannot help seeing my failure to achieve publication there as an indicator of my failure as a poet.

However, another side of me thinks differently. This side thinks there are many centres like raindrops falling on the surface of a pond. Each raindrop sends out ripples that overlap with ripples from other raindrops. Where is the centre? Each is a centre, and their centres interact with others, perhaps eventually reaching the far side of the pond.

Sometime in the 1970s, when I taught at Copenhagen University, I attended a reading in the English Department by Sorley MacLean. I don't think I had heard of him but we didn't have that many readings by poets so I went along. There were about a dozen of us, a poor turn-out MacLean must have thought, and perhaps a measure of his worth? (At about the same time, Seamus Heaney read to a packed audience in a large lecture hall.)

I am glad I went because it was the greatest experience of poetry I have ever had. MacLean talked about each poem, then read it, first in Scots Gaelic and then in his own English translation. He read with a keening tone in a way no longer used by poets but which was common to poets of his generation—R.S. Thomas had it to a degree, and you can hear it in the recording of 'The Lake Isle of Innisfree' read by W.B. Yeats. All the tragedy of Scots Gaelic was enfolded in those tones, a lament for his lost world of Raasay and for the young men with whom he fought and who he saw die in the desert campaign of the Second World War. His reading of the Gaelic sent cold chills down my spine in a way that had never happened before and has never happened since. The translations were illuminating, of course, and moving in their own way, but at the deepest level they were not necessary.

I have often thought about that afternoon. *There* was one such centre, in the Western Isles of Scotland ('remote' or 'far-flung' needs to be added if you are a metropolitan), and ripples from it had touched me deeply.

The idea of multiple overlapping centres of culture is particularly relevant to Wales, because we have never had a metropolis in the way the English have in London. Wales has always been decentred. It is true that Cardiff has become the official capital of the country and that political power now resides there. Culture, however, does not. Travel in Wales is easier today, but writers and artists are dispersed across the land in small towns and villages in a way that is not so different from how it was in the fourteenth century.

Seen from within the gravitational pull of the metropolis, this confirms the status of Wales as a backwater, and if you think in these terms then that is undoubtedly what we are. Didn't Dylan Thomas escape to London as quickly as he could? Didn't R.S. seek publication there? Dylan Thomas was always an outsider in London, though, and all his poetry and fiction is deeply infused with 'provincial' Swansea and West Wales. He succumbed to the gravitational pull of the English metropolis and it bought him fame, but at the price of helping to destroy him.

R.S. Thomas felt the pull but was only partially drawn in by it. He remained true to the source of his poetry in 'obscure' country parishes in Mid and North Wales. Visiting Sarn y Plas a couple of years ago— the tiny bwthyn built out of massive boulders overlooking Porth Neigwl where he wrote and his wife Mildred Eldridge painted—I peered through dusty panes at the emptied rooms, the bare floorboards. Here too had been a centre, a great centre. On the way north from Aberystwyth we also paid a visit to Hedd Wyn's family farmhouse, Yr Ysgwrn, now a museum in honour of the poet. There was another centre, one of the many that ripple and overlap in the formation of Welsh culture.

All of this will seem like special pleading, of course, if you subscribe to the metropolitan view of things, and there can be no arguing about this. I think I am right, however, even though it leaves me no clearer as to where I stand myself.

Democracy Betrayed

When the gap between rich and poor becomes outrageous, and when this coincides with economic smash-up, the result, more often than not, is revolt from below, as the dispossessed of the world seek revenge, if not redress, for what has been visited upon them. An aggressive levelling instinct emerges—'When Adam delved and Eve span / Who was then the gentleman?' the rebel priest John Ball asked, inciting the wretched of England during the Peasants' Revolt of 1381.

In the '80s Reagan and Thatcher preached the gospel of the 'trickle down' effect. Allowing the rich to become filthy rich was a *good thing* because immense wealth generated economic prosperity which percolated to the benefit of all. The Neo-Conservatives may have believed this, I suppose, but part of the trade of politics is lying, and it is equally possible that they sold this knowing it to be a big lie.

Forty years on, we face the consequences—immense riches hidden from prying eyes by a bewildering maze of shell companies based in mini-states that accommodate them; the corruption of politics through wealthy donations to party funds and behind-the-scenes lobbying; the decline of industry as global corporations close factories in one country to open them in another where labour is cheaper. Ordinary people have got very little out of this, because nothing much has 'trickled down' except the laughter of the rich as they show off their mansions and yachts in glossies like *Forbes* and *Hello!*.

Great disparity of wealth creates imbalance in political systems, especially democracies. Anger and resentment from below gravitate toward demagogic politicians who hold out promises of redress, who say the system is at fault, that it needs to be 'cleansed', that power must be seized, that democracy is broken. Enter Farage, Johnson, and Trump—the US must be freed from the Deep State, Britain must free itself from the EU to become a sovereign nation again. With them come unelected 'advisers' like Cummings and Bannon who want to destabilise the system, creating conditions for a libertarian alt-right power base. It is the first step toward abandoning democracy for 'dictatorship of the people' with a strong leader at the helm, as happened in Russia in the early 1920s and in Germany after 1933.

America, with its delusion of 'manifest destiny', has long believed that democracy (American-style) is the future, and for many this was confirmed by the collapse of the Soviet Union. With the demise of the only competing system, communism, we had reached the 'end of history' in Francis Fukuyama's triumphalist formulation. Other systems however are possible, as China has shown with its very effective capitalist economic structure controlled by a party dictatorship. In the new Russia, democratic processes are for show only, power residing in the hands of Vladimir Putin. It is in practice a dictatorship in which political opponents are jailed on trumped-up charges, and journalists and dissidents murdered by the state.

It is possible that in one hundred or two hundred

years, historians—if there are any—will look on the twentieth century as the 'Age of Democracy'. It will be part of the periodisation of historical studies, just as the feudal Middle Ages are for us. In the twelfth and thirteenth centuries the tripartite division of society into knights, priests and peasants, under the king, was divinely ordained. No other system was conceivable. In the same way, we in the West believe democracy is here to stay.

One should be distrustful, however, of assertions which place the speaker at the pinnacle of human achievement. It suggests special pleading which is likely to be overtaken by events, just as 'the end of history' was very quickly overwhelmed by history which, it turned out, was far from finished.

Political developments so far this century suggest the future may be demagogic and dictatorial, with democratic processes maintained as a façade. The trend will be toward the intolerant right, rather than the intolerant left. There will be a 'free press' but its influence will be eclipsed by powerful far-right channels like Fox News and through the dissemination of fake news on social media. Under such conditions, the police are likely to become an instrument of government, backed by military intervention where necessary. Trump's handling of Black Lives Matter protests and inner-city rioting may well be harbingers of what is to come, because Biden's victory, though welcome, is not the last word, and is unlikely to restore democratic politics to a society which is divided against itself in such manifest and bitter ways. The trend is not dissimilar in England.

The question—if one wishes to save liberal democracy—is what can be done about it?

Tribulations of a Meat-Eater

I have a problem with meat, which I have eaten all my life. During my childhood, meat was hearty—roasts, chops, steak, ham, liver, bacon, sausage, faggots. Meat was the centre of every meal, bought from my mother's preferred butcher in town, the meat displayed there on cool slabs of marble, later in refrigerated trays, the butchers always cheerful with rubicund cheeks, looking as if they enjoyed life, with badinage ever-to-hand for their housewife customers. The butcher's was a good place to go, despite the sweet-sickly smell from the meat which permeated the shop. I had no difficulty with that, nor with watching a scrubbed pig's carcass carried at shoulder height from a van across the street. Dismemberment denatures meat, it is not an animal, it is something else.

The trouble is the denaturing is false. Every time I walk to town these days, I pass through fields of grazing sheep. There is one particularly fine flock of black sheep, though they are not strictly black but a very dark brown, the colour of Java coffee. They are not as timid as white sheep, the ram, especially, with his curled horns, stands his ground, though he is wary, his body tensed, ready to turn and run if this human makes a move. Perhaps it thinks, if it thinks at all, that the fence is there to keep humans out, not sheep in. All the more shock, then, when the farmer comes with his dog and they are rounded up, crowded into a lorry and taken to the slaughterhouse. (Slaughterhouse being a more honest word than abattoir.)

From my earliest childhood I was used to seeing sheep at Abergavenny cattle market, packed in small pens, heads resting on the backs of their fellows. The auctioneer stood above them on a plank walkway. Below him stood the farmers, lean men in cloth caps from the Black Mountains, watching the auctioneer as he took bids at great speed. To the uninitiated it sounded like rhythmic verse—a *trobar clus* which only the troubadour-auctioneer and the farmers understood

There was the auctioning of cattle, too, though we never stayed for that, and outside the Butter Market canary-yellow chicks packed jostling in cardboard boxes like animated squeaking toys.

I accepted this as normal, which of course it was. Humans were on top, while animals were live products to be passed from farmers to the market to the slaughterhouse, then back to us via the butcher's, ending as roasted, fried, boiled meat on our table.

If you shake the kaleidoscope, however, you get a different picture. Then animals become the slaves of a superior species who possess power over life and death—but death always for the animals in the pens.

The slaughterhouse in Abergavenny was attached to the market, and if you walked past after the market was over you heard the melancholy lowing of the cattle, the wrenching squeals of the pigs, the baahing of the sheep, penned overnight awaiting death. And that smell again, stronger than at the butcher's. Evenings, strolling past, perhaps on the way home from the Coliseum Cinema, remain with me. I can visualise them clearly, though sound is harder to articulate in retrospect, except as a faint echo of the animals' fear and despair. I would need to be a great impersonator to give a sense of those sounds and I don't believe I could bear it.

Some years ago, there was an advert in one of the newspapers which affected me. It consisted of a photograph of a skip filled with pigs' heads, around which people with pig masks stood, hands raised to their cheeks in pig-horror. Shake the kaleidoscope and what seems normal becomes a nightmare. I visited a pig farm once in Denmark. It consisted of a very large shed filled with small pens containing perhaps two or three hundred pigs, many with piglets wriggling and suckling from their prone mothers' teats. The air was acrid with the stink of ammonia and rent with squeals and grunts. The farmer bred trout as well, and while I was there the fish were being transferred from one dam to another, propelled at great speed through a pipe which must somehow have sucked them up with the water, discharging them into their new quarters.

On the train from Aberystwyth to Shrewsbury you pass dozens of farms, many with outsized closed sheds. I know what is in them, battery-farmed chickens, or pen after pen of pigs, or cattle in stalls. Outside nothing stirs as the train rattles past, but inside, the air will be fetid and filled with the cries of animals deprived of all semblance of a natural existence.

When we go to the butcher's or the supermarket we don't usually think of this. Perhaps, even, we say we didn't know, just as many Germans said they 'didn't know' about the death camps at the end of the war. Not knowing is best until the wall of self-imposed ignorance collapses. Perhaps, too, factory-farming learned a thing or two from the camps? The methods are similar, only the species are different.

You can of course choose to eat free range and organic meat which is what we do, salving your conscience by thinking 'at least they had a good life in the fields'. The endgame, however, is the same.

Feeling as I do, I ought to give up meat, and I know there are sound environmental reasons for doing so. I do eat less and less of it but I enjoy cooking and selfishly there are too many meat dishes I like to cook and eat. I live therefore with the gap between the sheep I pass every day in the fields and the denatured lamb I dice for a curry. These are irreconcilables and I live by trying and failing to keep them apart.

Footprints in the Snow

By chance this Christmas we received two cards showing winter scenes by the Japanese artist Utagawa Hiroshige. The one is called *Snow at Benten Shrine at Inokoshira Pond.* The other is simply *Snow at Night.*

The first shows a bleak winter scene with three tiny figures making their separate ways to the shrine which is on a small island. All three appear to be male, the largest in the foreground is about to cross a bridge over the pond. There are two more bridges to the left, the nearest of which has just been traversed by the second figure. The third is mounting steps toward the doors of the shrine. The 'pond' seems more extensive, more like a lake.

Everything is still. Pine trees surrounding the shrine are freighted with snow. Reeds, stiff and frozen, protrude from the icy water. A light snow is falling from a uniformly grey sky which darkens at the upper edge of the picture. Toward the top right there are four columns of Japanese characters—1-3-3-3—and further to the right again a column of 3 characters, ending in a red stamped seal. The only colours are the blue of the pond and the brown of the wooden temple with a slightly lighter brown for the doors. The two figures approaching the steps one behind the other are also dressed in blue. They are wrapped up tight against the bitter cold—and perhaps I am mistaken about the nearest figure; perhaps he is walking *toward* us and away from the shrine—he is bent beneath a large

Japanese hat so that his head cannot be seen. Yes, I think he is walking toward us, seemingly unaware of the others' presence, focussed on the intense cold.

Snow at Night has a similar feel of winter chill. It is snowing more intensely here and a group of pines to the left are laden with heavy snow. Again there is a shrine, at least I suppose it is a shrine, with a gate and a fence of bright blue that adds to the sensation of freezing cold. We are closer to what is going on in this image, with the focus on four women, high-born I assume, richly and elegantly dressed. Two of them have just emerged from the gate, huddled together under an umbrella. They bend toward a third woman, also under an umbrella, who I think is about to go in. They are chatting about something. Their feet, we can see, are naked, teetering on double heeled sandals like tiny stilts. A fourth woman, who has already entered the precinct under her umbrella, is turning back to listen. More people have been here and snow at the entrance to the shrine is pock-marked by traces of many feet. The scene is animated by the women whose clothes are full of colour, who are vivacious and talkative.

The Japanese characters are at top left this time, again in four columns, but arrayed 2-2-1-3, and at bottom left a column of 3 characters above a red stamped seal.

When I was a child in the 1940s and '50s we always had snow in January or February and sometimes at Christmas. If it snowed overnight, the world looked newly created. Best of all the Deri, Rholben, Llanwenarth Breast, Sugar Loaf, Blorenge, Skirrid

Fach and Skirrid Fawr—all the hills surrounding the town—would be billowing sails above white fields, everything draped in the silence peculiar to snowy weather, sound reduced to the faint *swish* of a car driving cautiously with chains on its wheels; voices were small; everyone enlivened by the scene but huddled in winter coats for the cold.

That memory is revived for me in Utagawa Hiroshige's woodblock prints. But these are scenes you are not part of. You can only look on, as the men trudge to and from the shrine, as the richly attired women gossip at the gate. For all of them, you do not exist, have never existed, can never exist.

For the viewer, they do not exist either, any more than the footprints in the snow or the snow itself. The fine ladies, especially, remind me of a scene in Harry Martinson's space epic *Aniara* where the Mima—the mysterious half-animate computer that entertains the doomed occupants of the giant space ship with images snatched from across the galaxy—projects a picture of a woman beautifully dressed in the latest fashion as she strolls beside the sea. She deserves, the narrator says, to live forever unchanged, but

Tro inte det.
Den kvinnan är förmultnad
sen fyra millioner år och ingen,
ej ens den väldiga kulturkrets
som födde henne har satt minsta spår.

Do not believe it.
That woman decayed
four million years ago and no one
not even the great culture
that nurtured her has left the slightest trace.

Utagawa Hiroshige painted in the first half of the nineteenth century. He, the marvellously fashionable women, and the solitary men, are as much dust as the elegant woman whose brief vision beguiled the occupants of Aniara. Their väldiga kulturkrets has for the most part disappeared, too, overwhelmed by time and the influence of Western culture after the Second World War.

The White Man as Burden

As I have suggested above, much of my reading in the past ten years has been of eyewitness accounts of the nineteenth-century's wars, but I also read accounts by Victorian explorers, from Alexander Burnes' *Travels into Bokhara* to Henry M. Stanley's *In Darkest Africa*. Africa, especially, attracted me, and I progressed from Stanley to Mungo Park, Verney Lovett Campbell, David Livingstone, J.S. Jameson, Edmund Musgrave Barttelot, Herbert Ward, A.J. Mounteney Jephson, Slatin Pasha, Gaetano Casati, Emin Pasha, and others. I didn't have a specific aim but jumped, as it were, from stone to stone across the wide reaches of the nineteenth century.

I belong probably to the last generation raised on a diet of anti-Victorianism—epitomised by Lytton Strachey's *Eminent Victorians*—which held that the nineteenth century was a stuffy, narrow-minded, po-faced era that produced long novels and boring architecture. It was an attitude reinforced by my parents (born in 1902 and 1908) who had themselves been brought up by Victorians; for although they had moved on to become 'modern' in a 1930s' way, they carried nineteenth-century baggage of token respect for religion and a narrow brand of respectability which they tried to inculcate in my brother and myself after the Second World War. At Birmingham University where I studied English there was a finals paper on Victorian Literature, but I had been bored by the compulsory seminars on the subject and did the minimum amount of work—no doubt contributing to my poor degree.

What my undirected reading has made me realise is that my prejudice against the Victorian era was just that, a prejudice, founded on inherited attitudes and ignorance, and that in fact the nineteenth century was a fascinating, multifaceted, rapidly evolving period which could never be exhausted.

What I have written so far, however, is a diversion or preliminary to what I set out to say, which is that as I read more and more about European exploration and conquest around the globe, it began to dawn on me what an extraordinary, in fact unique, undertaking this was. Humans have always been explorers and conquerors since *Homo sapiens* first ventured out of Africa. In more recent times, Arabs traded as far as the East Indies taking their religion with them; in the nineteenth century Arab slavers working out of Zanzibar were penetrating central Africa from the east as Europeans were from the West.

What is extraordinary is the success of Western Europeans, first in exploring, then conquering and exploiting the peoples of almost every continent, failing only in China and Japan (though they tried) and in the vastness of Russia's eastern empire.

What is extraordinary, too, is the assumption that whites had the *right* to conquer these diverse peoples, and that if they resisted being exploited, and even enslaved, they could be treated with the utmost brutality and savagery. So it was with the genocide of the Herero people in German South West Africa whose population was reduced from 80,000 to something like 15,000; so it was in Tasmania, where the Tasmanian Aborigines were wiped out; and so it was for Native Americans as whites swept across the Great Plains, murdering as they went, though killing 'Redskins' was rarely seen as murder.

If your skin was brown or black, you were fair game for Europeans whose superior technology in the form of firearms meant they could take your land by force and keep it by force. Specious self-justification was invoked—the civilizing mission of the white man who brought Christianity to inferior people living in ignorance, the Bible travelling in the wake of the gun.

When the conquered behaved, they were often seen as having the mentality of 'children'. British officers in the army of the East India Company saw their sepoys in this way. As the insurrection spread in 1857, an extraordinary number of officers commanding native regiments believed that 'their' troops would remain faithful. Only when the burning, looting and raping began in their cantonments did they realise their mistake. Then the 'children' became 'devils' to be brutally put down and savagely punished.

Not all Europeans bought the self-serving deceit of empire of course. In England there was a vocal anti-imperial faction, and men like Roger Casement whose Congo Report and Diary of 1903 (both reprinted in *The Eyes of Another Race*) exposed the appalling atrocities committed in King Leopold's Central African fiefdom by whites for whom black people were less than cattle.

Nonetheless, for a majority in 'Britain' in the nineteenth century, the Empire was a good thing, something to be proud of. We were bringing the light of Christianity to the dark places of Earth, shouldering 'the white man's burden'. It is the Janus face of Empire, and as a child in the 1940s and '50s I experienced it in the unquestioned Empire loyalism of my parents, and in cinema newsreels which reported on the Mau Mau's brutal murder of 'innocent' white farmers in Kenya, or the atrocities committed by the Malayan National Liberation Army, the armed wing of the Malayan Communist Party, in its fight for independence. They never showed the vicious response of the British Army. (My cousin Geoff had a photo of a group of British soldiers holding up the severed heads of guerrilla fighters, given him by someone who had fought in Malaya. He wouldn't show it to me.)

There is a fashion at the moment for liberal guilt, apologising for slavery and almost anything else white Europeans can be accused of. Saying 'sorry' is easy, however, which is why politicians have latched onto it. But the world is as it is and the past cannot be undone. It is so partly as a result of the technological revolution in Europe in the eighteenth and nineteenth centuries. It was a unique conjunction of circumstances which gave Europe, for a while, mastery of the globe. What Europeans did would have been done by any other group of humans, however, if circumstances favoured them. What might the Golden Horde have achieved in the thirteenth century had the Mongols possessed rifles, tanks and artillery against primitive Europeans dependent on cavalry, spears and bows and arrows. Conquest, the wielding of power over others less able to defend themselves, is at the root of the collective history of nations and peoples.

Where Do We Go Next?

I cannot help feeling that humanity is heading for a smash-up. I don't mean in terms of environmental catastrophe—which for most people is reduced to 'climate change'. I mean a common-or-garden smash-up. It is seventy-five years since the end of the Second World War, and although there have been wars in the intervening years, including major ones like the Vietnam War, they have been limited geo-politically. There was the 'Cold War', of course, but that was an armed stand-off, not a war.

Seventy-five years is a long time in human terms—there were only twenty years between the First and Second World Wars. There is a sense now of unease in the world, of shock waves emanating from the grinding of tectonic plates. Trump and Johnson are manifestations of this, ex-TV personalities, habitual liars with no regard for truth, who have risen to power through the rage of those who feel themselves to be dispossessed.

It is not only an Anglo-American phenomenon. Poland, Hungary, Turkey, to name three, have fascistic regimes that gained power by means of democratic processes which they then proceeded to dismantle. History does not, indeed, repeat itself, yet it is hard not to feel a certain *déjà vu* and that we have been here before in the 1930s

It is tempting to see the present as the repetition of fascism as farce. Or perhaps popular revolution as farce, with the storming of the Capitol in Washington a bathetic version of the storming of the Winter Palace— several over-weight stormers dying of heart attacks while their fellows roamed the corridors with no idea what to do next. In the end they were persuaded to leave and their leader—soon-to-be ex-President Trump—was impeached for a record second time.

Although this was revolution as Grand Guignol, however, the story is not over. Hitler's attempt at a coup in 1923 also ended in failure, with a gaol sentence for the far-right agitator, who nonetheless emerged a decade later as the head of a Nazi dictatorship.

Boris Johnson, like Donald Trump, has a third-rate mind, promising to lead 'Britain' (meaning England) into a magic world where the English are a great nation again. Thanks to him, 'we' have freed ourselves from the shackles of union with Europe, and all these foreign johnnies had better take note.

This is as delusional as the deep-seated American view of itself as the beacon of liberty and democracy, a nation whose motives are of the purest, who the world looks up to and longs to emulate, yet a nation which has provoked almost every major war since 1945; propping up dictators where convenient; overthrowing democratically elected governments as it suits; using assassination as a tool of foreign policy; destabilising the Middle East probably for generations.

Politics in the West has rested on a foundation of lies and self-deceit for the past forty years. What was held out as the revolutionary promise of the Reagan-Thatcher years has not materialised, yet mainstream politicians remain committed to 'Reaganomics' as the only option. That foundation is cracking, and has been for some time. Through those cracks the red-hot lava of popular rage is extruding into society at large. It has produced an angry, swaying instability which demagogues like Johnson and Trump seized upon and manipulated, and it is not clear at all where it will end.

Escape into Technology

A distinguishing feature of *Homo sapiens*, at least for the past 50,000 years, has been our inventiveness. The minds of humans excel in the formulation of new concepts, new ways of doing things. We are excited by technology, and embrace change, partly because it brings self-evident advantages, but also because we are persuaded to do so. New technologies bring huge profits to the companies that develop and market them, and humans *en masse* go along with this, because another distinguishing feature of our species is the deep urge not to be 'left behind'.

Even if you do not wish to adopt a new technology, therefore, you often have no choice because it sweeps everything before it, leaving you at a practical and social disadvantage.

A further distinguishing feature of the species is that while new technologies tend to be neutral in themselves, they can be used by humans equally for good and malevolent purposes. A recent example is the development of the drone which can be used, for example, by fire fighters to assess the extent of a fire or damage to a building, but can also be used by the state to spy on protestors, to assassinate enemies, and to make 'surgical' killings that are rarely surgical, all operated by technician-killers sitting at computers thousands of miles away.

The development of 'social media' and the internet are other recent examples which have locked nearly all of us into new ways of communicating and accessing the world. The internet is a source of information on such a scale that we cannot truly conceive of it. The iPhone can be used to film evidence of police brutality or the horrors suffered by civilians in a war zone, it can be used to call people together for a political protest. But these media can also be used to promote the cruel baiting and threatening of people by 'trolls', and on the Dark Web anything goes from money laundering and the selling of drugs, to 'snuff movies' and child pornography.

Humans never draw back from perfecting a technology because we perceive how terrible its consequences would be. The most grievous example is the atom bomb. Niels Bohr, Albert Einstein and other physicists, warned against it from the beginning, but scientists rarely have a say in how their discoveries are developed or applied.

The potential of nuclear physics to produce the most powerful weapon ever known to humanity was at once taken over by the US military establishment and by a government prepared to use it against defenceless civilians in Nagasaki and Hiroshima, contrary to one of the most fundamental Laws of War, though the law—that civilians should not be deliberately targeted—had already been broken by Germany, Britain and America in the blanket bombing of London, Cologne Hamburg, Dresden, Warsaw, Tokyo and other cities.

The atom bomb, of course, was the far less powerful precursor of the hydrogen bomb. For decades after the Second World War, the USA and USSR faced off over nuclear arsenals sufficient to destroy life on Earth many times over. This was called 'deterrence' under the threat of 'mutually assured destruction', with the supremely ironic acronym MAD. Since no nuclear weapon has been used in war since 1945, it may be said that MAD worked. It wouldn't have, the argument goes, if one side had known the other was bluffing.

This is where the deeply unethical nature of MAD is exposed, because the *thought* of using the H-bomb, and the *certainty* of doing so under certain circumstances, is a moral outrage that undermines any faith we might have in the better side of our nature. Those weapons are still there with no guarantee that one day, in a war that is going badly wrong for one of the protagonists, they will not be used with terrible consequences.

The pace of technological change never pauses. The gurus of Artificial Intelligence are planning a generation of hyper-intelligent robots—it will happen because we can make it happen—and there will be a new Pandora's box to fling open on the world, with applications for untold evil as well as good—because that is the nature of who we are.

Our relationship to technology and its influence on our lives has been changing for some time, until it has to be asked: does technology exist for humans or do humans exist for the endless proliferation of technology? Advances in AI in the next twenty to thirty years may answer that question in ways we do not necessarily like.

Truth v. 'Truth'

Certain words which have been central to European culture—'honour', 'courtesy', 'principle'—have so fallen out of use they hang like threadbare regimental banners in cathedrals commemorating long-forgotten wars; more at home in Pre-Raphaelite paintings of Arthurian legend with squires in tights and ladies in wimples than the world we live in.

Other words, too, are in the process of being abandoned, or of changing their meaning in ways which make them meaningless. 'Truth' is one of them. 'On a huge hill, / Cragged and steep, Truth stands, and he that will / Reach her, about must and about must go', wrote John Donne in the seventeenth century. In the twenty-first century, truth is relative. It is what you say it is—very convenient for anyone who doesn't want to bother with the hard discipline of thought.

Americans didn't land on the Moon but faked it in a studio. According to conspiracy theorists this is the truth. But truth in this sense is 'truth' and should always be enclosed in quotation marks. The truth is, Americans did land on the Moon and the evidence for this is overwhelming.

Increasing numbers of people prefer 'truth' however. It is easier than John Donne's definition and more fun, and social media provide the forum for 'truth's' replication in millions of lazy minds.

'Fact' is another word the meaning of which is being tested to destruction. Facts, like truth, can be hard to verify, but facts exist. The principles of aerodynamics are well understood and are the same everywhere—that is a fact. There is no such thing as Christian or Islamic aerodynamics, though I would not be surprised if someone somewhere claims there is, because we live in a postmodern world of 'alternative facts', very useful to politicians for whom truth and facts are malleable pawns in the game of power and deceit.

'"When I use a word," Humpty Dumpty said in a rather scornful tone, "it means what I choose it to mean—neither more nor less."

"The question is," said Alice, "whether you can make words mean so many different things."

"The question is," said Humpty Dumpty, "which is to be master—that's all".'

Art in the Flatlands

There is a paradox at the core of high art culture. To be sustainable it requires a degree of social cohesion and stability. Writers need publishing houses, artists need galleries, composers and musicians, concert halls. All of this requires funding, whether from the state or from private patronage. It requires audiences, too, who have leisure and sufficient funds to buy books, paintings, attend concerts or theatre performances.

The paradox consists in the fact that great periods of artistic *production* often seem to emerge in times of social stress and dislocation.

The French Revolution, followed by the revolutionary and Napoleonic Wars and the fear of invasion and revolution in England, were major factors in the creation of the Romantic sensibility in the arts which produced the poetry of Wordsworth and Coleridge, who were themselves suspected for a time by the English government of being dangerous radicals and spies.

The political, social, cultural, and psychological crises resulting from the First World War were the forcing ground of Modernism, the attempt by Eliot, Pound and others to salvage something from the wreckage of Western civilisation, and at the same time to give expression to the dislocation and disorientation felt by many after 1918.

The Russian Revolution of 1917 and the chaos and brutality of the ensuing Civil War equally led to a great period of experimentation in the arts in Soviet Russia, with new ideas, new ways of seeing. Something similar happened in Germany in the crisis-ridden Weimar Republic.

If we look further back, the second half of the fourteenth century was a period of unparalleled crisis in England. The Black Death killed circa 1.5 million between 1348 and 1350 at a time when the country was already under stress from the Hundred Years War. One consequence was the Peasants Revolt of 1381. Yet these decades also witnessed an extraordinary flowering of English poetry. Geoffrey Chaucer produced his great innovatory poems *The Canterbury Tales* and *Troylus and Cryseyde*, while outside court circles there was a renaissance in alliterative poetry of outstanding quality—notably the anonymous *Sir Gawain and the Green Knight*, *Pearl*, *Patience*, and *Cleanness*, and William Langland's *Piers Plowman*. Chaucer's contemporary, John Gower, wrote poetry first in Latin and French, as many court poets did before him, but for his last great work, *Confessio Amantis*, he turned to English. Poetry in England had changed forever.

There are other reasons for innovation in the arts, of course, including the personal demons of the artist, and there are great upheavals which do not appear to have been the cause of new, dynamic movements in literature, music, or visual art. The Second World War seems to have been one such. It is not that there were no good artists in the period following 1945, but there was nothing comparable to the shifts in sensibility which produced Romanticism and Modernism.

Periods of stability, necessary for the dissemination of the arts, can be stultifying to the artists, as can the wrong kind of patronage, especially patronage by the state, which may begin as well-intentioned and necessary financial support, but ends by being a dead hand, in the sense of interfering in the direction of the arts by providing or withholding funding from projects of which the funding agency approves or disapproves. This in turn creates a situation in which the arts become servile in pursuit of that funding.

We are in such a situation in Wales now. State funded magazines plod on, state funded publishing houses produce the required number of books per year, some good, some even very good, but almost nothing which might take the Winter Palace by storm. The arts need money and are always short of it, but money supplied by the state becomes a means of control. Keydrych Rhys's magazine *Wales* was always chronically short of cash but while it existed it was independent, and influential beyond its limited resources. Ned Thomas's *Planet* which, in the 1970s, *did* run on a very small Welsh Arts Council grant, was openly nationalist and at times critical of the political status quo in Wales, to the extent that Welsh Labour did its best on at least one occasion to have it shut down. Today, it probably would be.

Caution is the word. There is no Keidrych Rhys now, no Caradoc Evans to be excoriated by *The Western Mail*. R.S. Thomas was the last poet to stir up outrage and hatred for his forthright views on Wales and to write great poetry out of the tension between Wales as he saw it and the visionary Wales of his dreams.

We need more writers with bite. We have lived in the flatlands too long.

The Masters of Infinity

In a recent edition of *The London Review of Books*, Tom Stevenson reviews two books about the militarisation of space. This is being led, naturally, by the USA which is in the process of establishing a 'space force' which will eventually have a staff of 16,000 and an estimated budget of $15.4 billion. A statement of intent, *Spacepower*, sets out what the new arm of the military will seek to dominate: 'orbital warfare, space electromagnetic warfare, space battle management, space access and sustainment, military intelligence and engineering/acquisitions.'

The space force is still mainly a project on paper, but it is based on a dream which American politicians and the military have had for several decades. Tom Stevenson quotes Lyndon B. Johnson from the late 1950s: 'Control of space means control of the world, far more certainly, far more totally than any control that has ever or could ever be achieved by weapons, or by troops of occupation... From space, the masters of infinity would have the power to control the Earth's weather, to cause drought and flood, to change the tides and raise the levels of the sea, to divert the Gulf Stream and change temperature climates to frigid.' The mad delusions of a Dr Strangelove.

Sixty years on, Johnson's 'vision' of the future has been overtaken by events in a savage, ironic way. We have discovered that we don't need American 'masters of infinity' to change the Earth's weather systems and raise sea levels from space. We don't even need them to divert the Gulf Stream and 'change temperature climates to frigid', because the Atlantic conveyor of warm water from the tropics is already under threat from the dumping of cold water at the poles. It is a pity Johnson is not alive to witness the alteration of 'temperature climates to frigid' this winter in his home state of Texas as a result of human-induced climate change—the would-be masters of infinity defecating, as it were, in their own backyard.

The US space force is nonetheless likely to become a reality with billions of dollars spent on it. So, as other countries like China and Russia seek to compete, we can look forward to a new Cold War in a narrow band of space at the outer edge of Earth's atmosphere.

The human mind seeks ever to expand, and there are visions of permanent bases on the Moon, even of terraforming Mars (though an article in *Nature* suggested this would take 50,000 years using current technology).

It is good that we cannot conquer spacetime. If it were possible, we would explore the many planets in our galaxy capable of supporting life, conquering and extirpating alien species as we went—especially if they were intelligent—because that is what humans do. Unless, of course, we encountered a species more rapacious and aggressive than *Homo sapiens*. Luckily, in galactic terms, the 'masters of infinity' are puny, so the only intelligent species we are likely to destroy is ourselves. For the rest of life on Earth that would be a positive outcome.

Poetry as Fly-Fishing

When I began writing poems in the mid-1970s, I also started to read widely in contemporary English-language poetry and immersed myself in the work of Ted Hughes, Sylvia Plath, Stevie Smith, Philip Larkin, William Carlos Williams, A.R. Ammons and many more. It seemed the natural thing to do, because otherwise you write in the dark, ignorant of what is being achieved around you. Some poets, like R.S. Thomas, I had been reading all along.

Inevitably this led to imitations, and I must have written hundreds of pieces of verse 'in the style of' these poets as I moved from one enthusiasm to another. They were all pastiches, of course, and soon abandoned. Those years were a prowling around, searching for a voice, for that is what all poets are after, ventriloquism being an important aspect of learning about rhythm, image, lineation, even punctuation; about how words can eventually be given the soft impress of your own voice. You learn more from failures than from your successes.

And most of this process is unconscious. In fact, it is best to keep the conscious mind out of it altogether. This is especially so in the *process* of writing. I have used the image elsewhere of fly fishing, casting a line over the placid surface of a lake. Around you is the living world, familiar, distracting, forever in motion. But that is not what you are after. You are after what is below the surface of the conscious mind. You can only cast your line and wait patiently, alert for that gentle tug which signals a bite. Hauled in, transferred swiftly onto the page, a poem is suddenly there, and if it is any good it will surprise you, even though you 'wrote' it. The surprise is that you could not have written it with your conscious mind. The poem's subject matter, images, rhythms, come from elsewhere. You, the 'writer', are the conduit.

Weeks or months later, there may be revisions, a word changed, a definite article deleted—'the' being a stumbling word in the English language; or you realise that the opening lines were a tentative entry into the real poem and have to be cut away. At other times, the attempt to excise a word, or add one, causes the whole edifice to collapse and the poem has to be abandoned. Periodically, you clean out the stables, pitchforking poems onto the muck heap. You never miss them.

The urge to write is with you every day but needs to be resisted. Too often the conscious mind takes over, deceiving you into believing that what appears on the page is genuine, whereas in reality it is fake. Gerard Manley Hopkins, I think, described such verse as Parnassian, written 'in the manner of' but dead at the core because it has been willed into existence.

As well as reading laterally among contemporaries, you also need a vertical, historical knowledge of poetry, to understand what has been achieved in the past. Here I was lucky, my BA degree syllabus gave me a good grounding in poetry in English from *Beowulf* to Thomas Hardy. When I began writing, I reread the Romantics, especially Wordsworth and Coleridge, because here was something I needed. I also read what was then known as Anglo-Welsh poetry, discovering poets like Glyn Jones, Harri Webb, Leslie Norris, and Alun Lewis.

It is useful, too, to read poetry in other languages. When I started to write, I had begun to learn Welsh, and read poems by T.H. Parry-Williams, R. Williams-Parry, Euros Bowen, and a few others. I also read poets in Danish and Swedish, notably Werner Aspenström and Harry Martinson. Later I discovered Knud Sørensen and read everything I could get by him. You learn a great deal about the language of poetry in this way, especially when making the attempt at translation, because you begin to intuit the magnetic forces which bind words in a poem together, and which are weakened or lost entirely in translation.

As one's own poetry advances, the need to read other poets diminishes, because you are no longer in search of models. Nor are you tempted to imitate. 'The effect of masterpieces on me, is to make me admire—and do otherwise,' Gerard Manley Hopkins again. Instead, you let your reading wander where it will. At the moment I am reading in translation the Russian novelists of the nineteenth-century. Certain writers I reread constantly—Joseph Conrad, one of the greatest poets, and Katherine Mansfield, another great poet who happened to write in prose. I might take down R.S., or Hughes or Larkin to reread a few poems, and read everything by certain poets I follow, like Ian McDonald and Knud Sørensen. But I don't feel impelled to read much in the vast outpouring of verse today, except odd volumes that come my way.

Occasionally I feel guilty about this—despite trying to write poetry, have I lost interest in it as a reader? The answer, perhaps, is yes and no. I rarely get excited by poetry now, except, paradoxically, by the prose poetry of Conrad and Katherine Mansfield where I often pause to reread a sentence or a paragraph for the rich texture of its rhythm and imagery. In the end, you have to be ruthless. You have to follow where your writing takes you, listening to its dictates. Academic specialists have to keep up with the field. Poets do not.

Where Is My Nation?

In a country like Wales that has been conquered, has had repeated attempts made to have its language suppressed, and been heavily settled in later years by descendants of the conquerors, it is common to find people measuring themselves and others against perceived standards of Welshness. For a long time—though it is changing now—many Anglophone South Walians were often bitterly aggressive toward the Welsh language, while Welsh speakers frequently looked down on monoglot Welsh speakers of English. Hence the bristling 'I'm as Welsh as you are' in the South, or 'He's proper Welsh' about a speaker of the language. (A version of the latter is, 'She speaks proper Welsh', indicating that the speaker feels that his or her demotic Welsh is inferior.) There are also divisions among Welsh-speakers between those who consider the Welsh of Gwynedd 'pure Welsh' as distinct from the 'less pure' dialect of the 'Hwntws', south of the Dyfi.

Coming from the south-east border town of Abergavenny, the question of Welshness has exercised me most of my adult life, though as a child growing up on the banks of the Usk, in the shadow of the Black Mountains, it never occurred to me. Why should it? I was who I was, the hills, the river, the town and its small gathering of people were where I belonged.

On the façade of the town hall, however, there was a large blue plaque proclaiming 'Abergavenny, Gateway to Wales'. A gateway opens in two directions, and the town could equally have proclaimed itself 'Gateway to England', which for many it was.

We were a mix of people in the 1940s and '50s, the majority working-class with a version of the accented English of the Valleys. At the other end of the social scale were the crachach (a word I didn't know then)— the town's solicitors, GPs, dentists, insurance brokers etc., with the shopkeeping class my parents belonged to squeezed in the middle. The town's working class were Labour while the bourgeoisie were Conservative. Most would have identified as 'British'.

And 'British' was a label made for my family. In the 1880s, my paternal grandfather emigrated from a Caithness crofting community to the Valleys, marrying a farmer's daughter from Somerset; my mother's family had moved to the Forest of Dean for the coal. Only in the Forest was there a hint of Welshness in the person of the Chartist leader Zephaniah Williams, who was distantly related. This had been hushed up, however, as it was considered an embarrassment and I never knew of the connection until my wife discovered it accidentally, talking with my mother. Jan Morris once referred to us borderers as mongrels, and that certainly applied to my family, though you would have to add 'British' mongrels.

I went through that gateway to university in England and spent nine years in Birmingham and Nottingham, something I find hard to believe now. It was an interlude in my life, if a long one, followed by thirteen years in Copenhagen. I was an alien in both countries which filled me with all kinds of discontent, though in Denmark, learning Danish, I began to question in a serious way for the first time who I was. On visits home, we would go to Cardiff to the Welsh Arts Council bookshop in Charles Street where I stocked up on 'Anglo-Welsh' and Welsh writers, getting near-first editions of Alun Lewis almost for the original cover price.

Back in my other home in Copenhagen, these were prizes, but prizes from another land. I was *learning* about a culture that should have been mine but which in my honest moments I knew was not. My patrimony was small, radiating from Abergavenny to Brecon, across to Hay, through the Llanthony valley to Pandy, and back along the old Hereford road to town. That was the only place where I belonged.

I cannot say that now, of course, because for the last thirty-six years I have lived near Aberystwyth. Everyone I knew in Abergavenny is dead and the town has changed, the natural world I absorbed as a child brutalised and in many cases destroyed. That is in the nature of things. When I go there these days, I feel that the town is both familiar and that I am a stranger.

Ceredigion is now my patch, stretching from Machynlleth in a narrow band along the coast to Aberaeron. It is here I have a circle of friends and where I use my stumbling Welsh among neighbours and in shops. As in Denmark, I belong but don't belong at the same time, unlike my childhood and youth in Abergavenny. Some of my friends here are English but have learned Welsh to such a high level that I think of them as Welsh, and certainly 'more Welsh' than me.

Since I walked through that gateway into England many years ago I became what you might call a twilight figure, flitting between identities, belonging to none.

The Relentless Cycle

Saccus stercorum, a bag of shit, that is what one fourteenth-century monk thought of the flesh. He had his mind on higher things, of course, the salvation of the soul and the beautiful-terrible array of God's plan for fallen humanity with Heaven's mansions a reward for the virtuous.

Conrad had a similar thought in a different way when in novels like *Almayer's Folly* and *An Outcast of the Islands* he described the virgin forests of Borneo as they were a hundred and fifty years ago, the massive trees wreathed in vines and tropical flowers, but thriving off the rot and dankness and gloom of the floor below. What seems so vibrant and beautiful living off death.

When you are young and healthy you don't think like this and ought not to. The body is something to rejoice in, to test to the limits of its capacity. That is a good time, the best in almost every way, because time unfolds, rich and green, and the whole of life is before you.

Viewed from the other end of the cycle it is different as the body weakens and its functions diminish. Nothing can be taken for granted then. There is no longer a green world spread before you but the looming edge of a precipice. That is how it has to be, because all life bows before time and the adamantine laws of evolution. When we dress the garden with blood-fish-and-bone meal, or dig in leaf mould, we acknowledge this, as if we were in Conrad's forests, or with the monk in his cell.

Saccus stercorum. I read his chronicle many years ago and cannot now remember the monk's name. He has been dead for six hundred years, part of the loam, of life's churning and recycling with no end other than the repetition of itself.

Money and Power

When I edited *Planet* I introduced an equal pay policy so that everyone who worked for the magazine received the same hourly rate. The only differential was in the number of hours worked.

This has always seemed to me the only fair way of distributing wealth. Why should a surgeon, a lawyer, a CEO receive more than a garbage collector, a sewage worker, a nurse? If any of the latter went on prolonged strike you would soon realise how important they are, garbage piled in the streets, a paradise for rats; sewers overflowing and polluting rivers and the sea; operations halted because there was no one to care for the patients. And if electricity workers struck, hundreds of thousands would die.

Society doesn't think like this of course. Differential rates of pay are 'natural', part of the 'reward' for expertise, an expression of one's position in society, a question of just deserts. But why? Surely the real reward for being a surgeon or a lawyer is the intellectual satisfaction of having learned rigorous and intricate skills, and in the case of a surgeon, certainly, of saving lives? A hospital is a huge hive and everyone who labours within it is essential to its viability.

So it was at *Planet*. I was the editor and had ultimate responsibility for the magazine and its contents, but it could not have been produced without the contribution of my colleagues. Why, therefore, should they receive less? Forty years of neoconservatism have made such a view laughable. Salaries of CEOs, 'celebrities', footballers, are often in their millions and very few seem to see anything wrong with this. It is, after all, a question of 'what the market will bear', of 'supply and demand'. Higher and higher go the incomes of the super-rich, as they become more and more adept at tax avoidance.

'For whosoever hath, to him shall be given, and he shall have more abundance; but whosoever hath not, from him shall be taken away even that he hath.'

Money is power and massive wealth a powerful corrupter, especially of politics. It seeps through the interstices of public life, the gleam of its gold corroding honesty, integrity and trust.

Varieties of Meaning

There are what might be called primary and secondary meanings in life. A secondary meaning is what gets you through the day, what you 'live' for, whether it is stamp collecting, bird watching, teaching, writing, the pursuit of political power, or the amassing of wealth.

The primary meaning, and there is only one, is the meaning of the universe and our place as humans within it. Since the Ancient Greeks at least, philosophers have puzzled over this, but philosophy is an arcane pursuit of specialists. The overwhelming majority have sought that meaning in religion, most notably the monotheistic religions of the Book, Christianity and Islam, whose proselytising zeal has carried these faiths to every corner of the globe. (Judaism is also a monotheistic religion of the Book, of course, but I discount it here because it is not a proselytising faith but one exclusive to Jews, and so limited in extent.)

What Islam and Christianity do is create a worldview in which humanity is placed at the centre of a great universal drama, with Allah/God the all-powerful director of our lives, meting out rewards and punishments according to our deserts. There is a clear beginning and a clear end, described and foretold in the Bible and the Quran. It is a belief system which billions have lived by in the past, as billions do today.

The trouble is the evidence for these 'self-evident' truths is underwhelming. People will go on believing them and living by them, of course, but the truth as revealed by cosmology, and at the other end of the scale, evolutionary biology, is that the primary meaning of the universe is that it has no meaning. It simply is. Implacable, vast, silent. And here we are, with the agony of consciousness that seeks above all significance for our brief lives. Happy the Christian or the Muslim.

The reality is that we are prisoners of spacetime and if we step beyond our self-created secondary meanings, seeking consolation in religion's hope of salvation in the beyond, we step not out of time, but into delusion. What to do? The answer is some form of Conradian stoicism. To live richly among our secondary self-created meanings, while recognising them for what they are. To face without flinching the nullity of the great void.

Sauve Qui Peut

The panic is on. And not on. TV news increasingly covers environmental disasters around the globe—flash floods, forest fires, hurricanes, glacial melt, species loss, pollution of oceans. Impossible not to be aware of it and the deepening crisis these events portend. And yet. Walking into Aberystwyth yesterday, the first day of the easing of lockdown, the road into town was one long stream of cars, vans, lorries, most of the cars with a single occupant. And people can't wait, in their millions, to travel again, to the Mediterranean, the USA, the Caribbean, South-East Asia, Australia, Chile, Peru. Can't wait for the return of cheap flights, cheap hotels, glittering sea and sandy beaches, suntans and pina coladas. Paradise regained after more than a year of restrictions caused by a virus, invisible to the human eye, that spread so rapidly and paralysed the powerhouses of capitalism. It could be an opportunity for change, and we all want to put a stop to global warming, pollution, species loss. Don't we? Well, yes. But not now, and not change that will affect our daily lives. As a neighbour said to me, 'You can't manage without two cars these days, can you.'

13/4/2021

Embracing Delusions

My uncle, Don Barnie, volunteered in the First World War and joined the Royal Welch Fusiliers. Deployed to Gallipoli, he had with him a cheap pocket diary for 1916 in which he made sporadic notes: '10 yds from the Turks trench. Bomb dodging.' He got out of that fiasco alive and was re-assigned to Mesopotamia, sailing through the Suez Canal and the Red Sea to Basra where he bought a small leather wallet, embossed 'Basrah 1916' in gold. Also stamped directly into the leather, and just visible, is a number, '13280', his identity number, and beneath it '8.th. R.W.Fus.'.

On the 17th of February he was promoted to sergeant, and his unit set out as part of the relief force sent to raise the siege of Kut-al-Amara. Don wasn't a great writer and the diary entries are few and far between: 'Sheikh Saad'. 'HOSTILE. ARABS.' 'Pouring with rain (mud)'. And then on Wednesday, the 5th of April, 'We charge Big Battle. Wounded Bullet [word illegible] bandage'. And that was the end of combat for Don. He was transported on a hospital ship to India: 'Arrive at Bombay, Fine Place. Colaba Hospital.'

The Basra wallet saved Don's life. Kept in the left-hand pocket of his combat jacket it diverted a Turkish bullet an inch away from his heart. I have the wallet, torn at the lower left corner where the bullet passed through.

Don didn't leave much when he died, but among his effects which I eventually inherited there is an anonymous poem, 'Farewell', on a sheet of A4 card. At first glance it appears to be handwritten in an elegant script on a crudely painted sandy yellow background, but in fact it is printed. Don certainly would not have written the poem. He must have bought it—in India, perhaps—because it expressed what he felt about his experience. The poem ends:

Farewell, ye land of heatstroke
Farewell, O Basrah Rash
Farewell, O Barren desert
Farewell, ye treacherous clime
Farewell, ye land of pestilence
Farewell, to Shatt-al-Arab
Euphrates, Tigress too
and I hope O Mesopotamia
that I've seen the last of you.

A little under a hundred years and British troops were back, supporting America in one of its neo-colonial wars. The names on the map had changed—Mesopotamia was now Iraq, Basrah had dropped its 'h'. No doubt the army of occupation assigned to hold the Basra Governorate in 2003 had better conditions than Don's Royal Welch Fusiliers in 1916, but as the occupation faltered and the Brits found themselves bogged down in a guerilla war they were losing, many soldiers must have echoed the sentiments in 'Farewell'.

England has never got over its two World Wars. The First was the last time it fought as a major imperial power. It claimed to do so again in 1939-45 and has lived off legendary interpretations of Dunkirk, 'standing alone', and D-Day, ever since, winning the war single handedly, with a little help from the Americans. The truth of course is that Soviet Russia won the war on the Eastern Front, while the second front in Normandy could never have been launched without overwhelming American manpower and matériel.

Britain's days as a world power ended there. The trouble is, too many are unable to accept that we inhabit an island with a moderately strong economy off the coast of continental Europe, and that our history has followed the trajectory of other European empires—the Dutch, the Spanish, the Portuguese—from a period of great wealth and dominance based on colonial conquest, to sharp decline once those colonies were lost.

The fiasco of Brexit owes much to people clinging to this myth of British greatness. Only free ourselves from the shackles of the European Union and we'll put the 'Great' back in Britain. We will trade with the world, 'punch above our weight', 'stand shoulder to shoulder' with our American 'cousins', with whom we have a 'special relationship'.

All of this is delusion. During the referendum campaign a TV news vox pop interviewed an old man who said trade after Brexit would be no problem because everyone in the world 'loves us'. Don's son, my cousin Geoff, saw this too. He was a merchant seaman from 1944-48 and had sailed around the world. 'No they don't,' he said, 'they bloody hate us.'

The puffed-up sense of the UK's importance in the world was encouraged by Boris Johnson who fancied himself as a Churchill, destined to lead the people of 'Great' Britain into a new dawn. But Johnson is a glove-puppet Churchill and Britain a glove-puppet 'great power'. The RAF is still good to bomb the citizens of countries we invade who have no air power themselves, but the Army lost two wars in Afghanistan and Iraq, and the Royal Navy is a shadow of what it was. The recent threat to send our latest aircraft carrier to the South China Sea to 'show the flag' and deter the Chinese was a joke.

So here we are, cut loose from Europe, our main trading partner, scurrying in search of favourable trade agreements, placing our hopes on a deal with the USA, unmindful of the fact that America holds all the cards.

Collapse

The world's leaders are waking from their slumber to acknowledge that the climate is veering out of control and that if steps are not taken now to reduce greenhouse gas emissions we will very soon reach a tipping point. But what if this is impossible? What if our species' brain has not evolved to cope with a crisis of such complexity and on such a scale?

It is already clear that nothing can be the same again. Refugees and economic migrants from Africa and the Middle East are changing society in Europe, as refugees and migrants from South and Central America are changing the USA. It is only a beginning. As conditions deteriorate, the now prosperous West will experience an overwhelming surge of displaced people. Patrol boats and walls will be of no avail. Society will have to adapt and change, and culture will change with it. What we think of as the great inheritance of European art, literature, music, thought, will be largely irrelevant because it does not address the new world in which we will have to live.

The idea of reducing carbon emissions to zero has behind it the assumption that, if successful, we will be able to continue our lives as before—with adjustments. Perhaps we will all have to drive electric cars, for example, but there will be cars nonetheless. This is unlikely, however, because we are in the process of crossing one of the great Rubicons in the 3.8-billion-year history of life on Earth, mired in a self-created mass extinction which may approach the one at the Cretaceous-Tertiary boundary 65 million years ago. The Earth is so overpopulated with humans that even if all nations reached zero carbon emission by 2030 or 2040 our demands on the Earth's resources would still cause ecological collapse.

The world's governments should therefore be planning now for the worst-case scenario, deciding which low-lying coastal areas to abandon, which to try to save with substantial sea defences. The coasts of Bangladesh, Florida, Louisiana would have to be systematically evacuated. Much nearer home, Aberystwyth could probably be saved with strengthened and heightened sea walls, but the village of Borth to the north, much of which is at or below current sea level, would have to be abandoned and large tracts of reclaimed pasture land in the Dyfi estuary allowed to revert to salt marsh. Perhaps tropical forests could be regenerated in some way, though probably not. And what to do about desertification, the steady advance of the Sahara into the Sahel? Nothing perhaps because it may be unstoppable. Freshwater supplies will be a huge problem and money should be poured into research into desalination technology to make it less costly and more energy efficient.

Chaos is what is most likely to happen, however, with savage wars between states for land and resources, and to prevent themselves from being overrun. There will be attempts at global co-operation but they are likely to fall apart as the Earth's ecosystems collapse. We are entering Judge Dredd territory not a world where the lion lies down with the lamb.

The False Shepherd

The Lord is my shepherd; I shall not want.
He maketh me to lie down in green pastures:
he leadeth me beside the still waters...

Everyone knows these opening lines of Psalm 23, or used to. I intoned them as a child in the grey vaulted light of St Mary's Church in Abergavenny. The lines have a comforting feel to them—the Shepherd will guide you, you can lie down securely in green pastures because He is there to watch over and protect you.

Only recently did it occur to me that there is something wrong with this image. A good shepherd will naturally take care of his flock. He will see that they are fed and watered, and will protect them from predators. But that is only the beginning of the story.

Why does a shepherd do this? It is because he is husbanding his sheep with a view to them being slaughtered for meat, and since in the psalmist's day butchering would have been according to ritual, the animals' death would be slow and agonising. The sheep are ultimately of interest to the shepherd for what they provide, which is either food for his extended family or tribe, or profit in the marketplace.

David, to whom the psalm is attributed, didn't think his metaphor through to the end, truncating it to give a false sense of security. On the internet there are hundreds of images of stained-glass windows depicting Jesus cradling a lamb in one arm and hold a shepherd's crook in the other, or Jesus surrounded by a trusting flock, and when you enter a church and view one of these, with light streaming through the blue, red, and green glass, with a golden halo around the Saviour's head, it is hard not to be filled with a sense of peace.

Christianity, however, is very much a religion of blood and by a clever sleight of hand Jesus becomes the lamb, the innocent who was butchered on the cross in Revelation 7:14. To be saved we must be among those who 'have washed their robes, and made them white in the blood of the Lamb'. It is a piece of magical thinking: the sheep now bathe in the shepherd's blood, and the roles of the shepherd and his flock are reversed.

All those stained-glass images of the Shepherd cradling an innocent, defenceless lamb are just one side of the coin, because the green pastures leadeth not only to still waters, they lead also to the slaughterhouse and the slitting of throats. The poet David wrote with a mask on, and we never see his face.

Down Among the Struldbrugs

In *Gulliver's Travels*, Gulliver journeys to Luggnagg where he learns of the existence of the Struldbrugs. They are immortal as a result of a rare genetic mutation. How marvellous, Gulliver thinks, what wisdom you would acquire, what intelligent conversations you would have with fellow Struldbrugs, what advice you could impart to princes and kings.

Gulliver's guide quickly disabuses him. Until they reach eighty they age like everyone else, but after that it as if they are left behind in a world that moves on without them: 'They have no remembrance of any thing but what they learned and observed in their youth and middle age, and even that is very imperfect... The least miserable among them, appear to be those who turn to dotage, and entirely lose their memories; these meet with more pity and assistance, because they want many bad qualities which abound in others.'

When they reach eighty, the guide continues, 'they are looked on as dead in law', and their heirs inherit, only a 'small pittance' being kept back for their support. From then on degeneration is progressive: 'At ninety they lose their teeth and hair; they have at that age no distinction of taste, but eat and drink what ever they can get without relish or appetite. The diseases they were subject to, still continue without increasing or diminishing. In talking, they forget the common appellation of things, and the names of persons, even of those, who are their nearest friends and relations. For the same reason, they never can amuse themselves with reading, because their memory will not serve to carry them from the beginning of a sentence to the end; and by this defect, they are deprived of the only entertainment whereof they might otherwise be capable.'

'The reader,' Gulliver muses, 'will easily believe, that from what I had heard and seen, my keen appetite for perpetuity of life was much abated.'

Swift is remarkably prescient of where we are today, with an ageing population and an archipelago of care homes, rest homes, nursing homes—call them what you like—where the aged who can no longer look after themselves are housed. They may not be 'looked on as dead in law', but life savings are taken to pay for their care, homes are frequently sold, a life's possessions disbursed. We have created a new kind of gulag, well intentioned, certainly, and out of necessity, but a gulag all the same, where modern-day Struldbrugs are confined until released discreetly in an undertaker's coffin.

The War-Making Species

In the debate about how to reduce greenhouse gas emissions and avert a global climate disaster, emphasis is placed on agreements and commitments, the nations of Earth coming together in a spirit of co-operation, recognising that we face a common danger. As the crisis deepens, some of these agreements and commitments will no doubt hold, but there is a problem which I do not recall being discussed very much: that at a crucial level international politics are still conducted as if we lived in the nineteenth century.

This is especially true of the 'great powers', America, China, and Russia, who think in terms of spheres of influence, power blocs, and economic and military dominance, as they challenge one another for global hegemony. The Cold War between America and the USSR lasted half a century. It involved a devastating arms race, with America spending at least $5.5 trillion on nuclear weapons alone. Now a similar cold war is developing between America and China, with perceived American weakness encouraging China to expand its military presence in the Pacific at the same time as its economic growth challenges America's faltering economy. The US has responded by creating alliances with South Korea, Japan, Australia, and India in an effort to contain Chinese ambitions.

China also threatens Taiwan which it claims as an indivisible part of its territory. It is far from certain what America would do if there were an invasion from the mainland and Taiwan defended itself vigorously, which it would almost certainly do. The flashpoints of war may well be switching to the Pacific.

This is the double bind of humanity's attempts to avert ecological disaster. On the one hand, President Biden re-engages with the international community in the effort to reduce greenhouse gases; on the other, he builds military-economic alliances in the old way, determined to maintain America's global dominance.

A great power needs an Enemy, and if there is not one to hand, like Nazi Germany, it invents one, à la *1984*. For America it was the USSR and Communism; then militant Islam; and now China—as well as renewed hostility toward Russia. The Enemy justifies the billions of dollars spent each year on arms and the armed forces. It justifies American claims to be the defender of the 'free world', with military bases spread across the globe.

All empires collapse in the end, and the medieval image of the Wheel of Fortune, with princes rising to the top of the wheel, then tumbling to their downfall, is as relevant today as it was in the fourteenth century. All empires also delude themselves that they are different; that their dominance is ordained and without precedent. America's 'Manifest Destiny' is merely the latest incarnation of this flattering form of self-deceit.

If the twentieth century was 'America's century', then the twenty-first is likely to be China's. Trump's MAGA posturing was one sign of this, the whale thrashing in the shallows, mighty, and still dangerous, but dying. Whoever's century this is, however, the persistence of nineteenth-century ways of thinking about international relations is a rockfall in the road we need to travel if we are to ameliorate the worst effects of mass extinction and ecological collapse—it is already too late to think of reversing them.

I have never seen a figure for how much wealth the nations of the Earth have spent on arms since 1945, nor how much ecological damage has been caused by war upon war. Perhaps it is incalculable. Had that wealth been spent wisely, the world would now be a different place. But that is to speculate idly. Mankind is the war-making species and will continue to be so.

It is tempting to cast around for alternative visions that might point to a different way of organising societies and their relations with one another. The teaching of Jesus surely offers such a vision—of peace and fellowship, of turning the other cheek; a world where differences would be negotiated rationally and armies disbanded. The problem is that while individuals can strive to live by the New Testament, I can think of no state that has ever done so. Rather, the state invokes God to justify its aggressive policies, with fighting bishops like the Danish Bishop Absalon in the thick of it in the Middle Ages.

If in later ages the Church didn't take up the sword itself, it readily blessed those who did, with the absurd consequence that during the First World War priests on both sides blessed their respective nation's troops in the name of the same God before they went out to kill each other.

Where, then, to turn? How to reconcile the

irreconcilable? 'War is a mere continuation of policy by other means,' wrote Carl von Clausewitz almost two hundred years ago. There is little evidence to suggest that this will change any time soon.

3/6/2021

No Bribes Here

On the bus in town I watched a young woman scrolling down on her iPhone while negotiating her fare with the driver. She couldn't turn it off even for one minute to have a direct relationship with another person. Many of those who are part of the 'digital generation' are slaves like this to their machines.

On the other hand, another young woman in black punk gear, walked up the isle of the bus with a T-shirt which read 'Save the badger, cull the rich'. I had just read a book about badgers, and coincidentally an article on a naturalised Russian construction entrepreneur who had donated £1,000,000 to the Conservative Party. Shortly afterwards, his company was awarded a big Government contract. The entrepreneur and a Government spokesman claimed that this was entirely fortuitous—the £1 million was not a bribe but a donation given without thought of a quid pro quo. Nobody believes them, of course, but it doesn't matter, because cynicism, lying, and clientism are built into the system of Conservative government under Johnson. The lies are told with a flourish, without blinking, because they know they will get away with it.

The book about badgers made it clear that the case for culling these animals on the grounds that they transmit bovine TB to cattle is at best unproven. The case for 'culling' the rich, however, has plenty of evidence to support it.

Facing the Bottleneck

Who, if anyone, might survive the current mass extinction? My bet would be the !Kung San of the Kalahari and Aborigine tribes of the Australian desert, people who are used to surviving under the harshest conditions. They would be in the company of hardy generalists like crows, and (to our mind) less attractive species such as rats, cockroaches. There would be other species too, of course, though if 60 to 65 percent of species become extinct, as many evolutionary biologists and ecologists predict, there is no knowing which ones may squeeze through the bottleneck.

Each mass extinction in the geological past has exhibited features unique to itself; the uniqueness of the present one is that it is caused by one species, *Homo sapiens*. Mass extinctions often take thousands of years to unfold—a long time to us, but a blink of an eye in evolutionary terms. The great meteorite impact at Chicxulub 65 million years ago was an ultimate cause of the mass extinction at the K-T boundary, but it appears that species across many genera were already in trouble for several thousand years before that.

The present extinction event may unfold far more quickly because of its species-driven cause. As conditions on Earth worsen, the 8 billion humans are most likely to exploit the environment's dwindling resources ever further in a desperate effort to survive. It is right to hope that the nations of the Earth will come together in a way in which they have never done before in order to avert such a disaster. But this is counter to how our species evolved during 200,000 years. For millennia it has been natural to think in terms of one's family, related family groups, and one's tribe. In modern times this has been extended to the nation, united by common bonds of territory, language, culture, and religion. It is a long jump from here to what would in effect be world government if we are to slow, let alone reverse, the current extinction process.

Responses to the Covid-19 virus are instructive here. Since the pandemic is global, it makes sense to organise a global response. Vaccines should not be patented by pharmaceutical companies in the name of profit but delivered freely to the Earth's population. In this way the virus could be contained and perhaps eradicated. For the first eighteen months of the pandemic, though, wealthy countries like Britain and America were buying up doses of the various vaccines and even hoarding them while the poor of the Earth were left to fend for themselves. That is beginning to change with President Biden's announcement that the US will donate half a billion doses to countries that desperately need them. Half a billion is a lot, but it is estimated that 11 billion doses will be needed for effective worldwide vaccination. At the time of writing, 2 percent of the population of Africa have been vaccinated.

Just before Biden's announcement at the G7 Conference, Johnson's government let it be known it was cutting Britain's overseas aid budget by £4 billion, on the grounds that the cost of the response to the pandemic means the money is needed at home. As aid agencies have pointed out, thousands will die as a result but they won't be in Britain. Johnson will have expected protests but he also knew he would get away with it because the overseas aid budget is resented by many who have what might be called a *Daily Mail* mentality. False-footed by Biden at the G7 and not to be outdone, Johnson rapidly announced that Britain would be donating 100 million 'surplus' doses. The EU, too, has committed to 100 million. A proposal that patents on vaccines should be temporarily lifted to enable production in poorer countries has been resisted by the pharmaceutical companies and by the UK and other governments.

The evolutionary development of our species leads inevitably to thinking in terms of national self-interest first—charity begins at home, as the saying is—because in our deep historical past it was the most effective means of organising individual and group survival. There have been attempts to counter atavistic human attitudes in the past seventy-five years with the founding of the United Nations and the World Health Organisation, though both are under constant attack from one side or another, while the UN has been routinely manipulated in pursuit of national and ideological interests. Perhaps the ideal of the founders of the UN will win out as the crisis deepens. Perhaps it will not.

The times are desperate, yet from a certain perspective they are also extraordinarily interesting. Palaeontologists uncovered the five previous mass extinctions by piecing together an array of disparate evidence. It is one of the great feats of biological and geological science, but these events occurred in a past so distant that the human mind can barely conceive of them: 65 million years ago—try imagining that, year after year after year. *Homo sapiens'* mere 200,000-year existence is so brief that had we lived, say, 100 million years ago, it would be very difficult to date accurately the thin stratum where we had our brief existence, dating to within half a million years, plus or minus, being considered a good result in geology and palaeontology. And of course there was no species in Cretaceous or Permian times which could have observed and made a record of the thousands of years of decline leading to extinction. We know of previous extinction events, as it were, from a great distance seen through the wrong end of a telescope.

Now we can witness a mass extinction from the inside and chronicle it in detail. I do this myself in a small way, noticing each summer which insects are present in reasonable numbers, which are dwindling, and which seem to have gone forever. I do the same with birds, and make a note as to which tree species are succumbing to disease or environmental stress; which wild flowers are now rarities, which are taking advantage of the situation to flourish and spread.

This is a mass extinction which will be recorded like no other. You might ask what is the point? The answer, I suppose, is that we are a curious species, we need to know and understand, and derive immense satisfaction from the process of doing so. From this perspective it matters little if our species fails to make it through the extinction bottleneck. If this is to be our fate, then we can perhaps launch our findings in a sealed container on the immense sea of time that is to come before the sun exhausts itself. Intelligent life like ours is probably vanishingly rare, but who knows what species might evolve in the aftermath of our self-destruction, or what alien species might one day visit the Earth and try to puzzle out what happened here.

Cinema of Dreams

I have been surprised in the past by the number of English people who have told me they abhor nationalism and the one thing you can say about the English is that they are not nationalistic—surprised because the English are among the most nationalistic peoples I have come across.

This must be a function of empire. At its height the English Empire covered huge swathes of the globe. As a child I pored over a political map of the world in Mercator's projection. Pink for the Empire dominated—India, Australia, New Zealand, Canada, large tracts of Africa, most of the West Indies, Malaya, Borneo, on and on it went. The sun 'never set' on the Empire, as my mother used to repeat with pride.

Empire means conquest, however, and conquerors despise those whom they conquer. The masters look into the eyes of the vanquished as in a mirror wherein they see their own superiority.

The 'explorers' of Africa, and the soldiers, missionaries and settlers who followed, rarely considered that Africa was a populous continent where they had no business. Africans were another 'resource', to be exploited like hardwood trees of the primeval forest, gold, diamonds, rubber. Africans could be enslaved and shipped in their hundreds of thousands to North America, to the West Indies, to Brazil; they could be turned off their traditional land to become labourers on the vast estates of the whites. If you were a missionary, Africans had to be saved, led out of their primitive darkness. And they should accept all this with gratitude. As a Rhodesian plantation owner said on a BBC news bulletin, during the insurgency that led to Zimbabwe and independence, 'They've had a fair crack of the whip'—irony being in short supply at the time.

Loss of empire after World War II was a trauma from which the English have yet to recover. They still believe in England's 'greatness', sometimes in 'Great Britain's' when they want to include the Celtic 'fringe'. It is tacitly understood, however, that politicians like Boris Johnson always mean England.

It is as if the English are shut in a cinema sometime in the 1950s. A Pathé newsreel shows their lads fighting communist insurgents in Malaya, combatting cruel Mau Mau in Kenya; a young Queen Elizabeth waves to crowds of adoring black faces in Accra, to 'Aussies', 'down under', everywhere being 'down under' viewed from the high ground of England. Then they settle to the main feature which relives the glory days of the Battle of Britain or the Dam Busters—the French have failed again, the evil Germans are on the verge of conquering the world. Only the English stand firm. (Somewhere far, far away is the Eastern Front and the Russians…)

But all this is happening in a cinema dream of yesteryear, it is not happening now, and when the crowds pour out at the end of the show, they are faced with reality—empty shops, zero-hour jobs, abandoned factories, dilapidated northern cities and towns, the poor getting poorer, the rich laughing their way through shell companies to conceal their wealth and have it all to themselves.

And then there is the military. England used to be very good at colonial war. In the nineteenth century there was always a war somewhere in the Empire, the Army giving the Ashanti what-for, 'pacifying' the Raj after the Indian 'Mutiny', putting the Emperor of Abyssinia in his place. In this century, despite hi-tech weaponry, the Army was unable to hold Helmand against the Taliban or Basra against al-Sadr and assorted insurgents in aggressive wars of England's choosing.

What happened to 'greatness'? It cannot have been lost simply because empires decline and fall, leaving only the rump, like Holland and Portugal. It must be because England was betrayed. There has to be a scapegoat, and luckily there is one to hand—the European Union.

All that was missing was a charismatic leader, an English King Arthur, who would strike off the nation's chains enabling it to rise, a Leviathan again. And the man was there, in the person of Boris Johnson who told the English, or a good half of them at least, what they wanted to hear. To Trump's 'MAGA', Johnson trumpeted 'MEGA'.

This is egoistic, bombastic nationalism of the worst kind, yet many cannot see it. Some years ago, during a stop-over at Piarco Airport in Trinidad, I found myself in the company of several dozen English people on their way home from holidaying in the Caribbean. They were drunk, garishly dressed, and loud-mouthed, and took possession of the tiny departure lounge as if it was theirs. I was on my way back from Guyana where the quiet courtesy of the people I met made an embarrassing contrast. An Estonian poet acquaintance has told me that in Tallinn, a popular destination for English stag and hen parties, the English are disliked for their drunken, rowdy, arrogant behaviour in the bars and streets.

At the other extreme, when I was in Budapest to give a reading, a young Hungarian woman who worked for the British Council, told me that her English colleagues made her feel a foreigner in her own country. I had met some of them earlier—well-dressed, well-educated young men with the right accent, very self-confident, very English middle class. A hundred-and-fifty years ago, they would have been sent out to India or to the Gold Coast as colonial administrators.

The English cannot see themselves as others see them. That is admittedly a hard thing to do, but they rarely even try. They cannot see their history as anything other than admirable and glorious. This is being challenged now by Black Britains—would anyone call themselves Black English, I wonder?—but the process is slow, and very many English people retain a sense of entitlement and superiority wherever they go, so certain that they are the best, the envy of the world.

The Island

I have a fantasy of R.S. Thomas and Sorley Maclean not being dead at all but alive on a distant uninhabited island—St Kilda would do—where they write poems in their stone bothies, watch birds and listen to the waves, meeting in the evening to talk quietly and read what they have written to each other. The world does not know they are there and their poems will never be read by anyone else, but they don't care.

Dance of the Mayflies

A review by Priyamvada Natarajan in the *New York Review of Books* gives an overview of cosmologists' current thinking about the universe. It contains facts which can only really be understood mathematically, such as that neutron stars are the densest form of matter so far discovered, 'with about 1.4 times the mass of the Sun packed into a radius of just six miles'. How to comprehend this? An example is given: 'A teaspoon of neutron star material would weigh ten million tons.' The mind understands but does not understand. Neutron stars of the kind known as pulsars spin 'at incredibly rapid rates, close to a thousand times per second'. Try relating this to what we consider the reality of our everyday world. You realise that you cannot.

Then there is the fate of the universe. Cosmologists have mapped out five different scenarios, the most likely, it seems, being the Big Crunch, 'in which our current cosmic expansion reverses and the universe condenses into a black hole—a singularity'. The other is Heat Death, 'in which the universe expands forever, getting darker and more desolate'. If it is to be the Big Crunch: 'Having flipped course, a contracting universe would become an extreme place—heating up to incredibly high temperatures and densities, beyond anything we can produce in the laboratory.'

As Priyamvada Natarajan notes, what appears to be the inevitable death of the universe one way or another need hardly worry us. In about five billion years the Sun will have exhausted itself. 'As its core contracts, its outer layers will expand, passing into what is referred to as the red giant phase. At this point, its radius will have grown so large that it engulfs the orbit of Mercury. It will continue to collapse, ultimately leading to the formation of a dim remnant, a white dwarf, with fusion no longer supplying energy in the core.'

Priyamvada Natarajan doesn't say (or need to say) that all life on Earth will have ceased to exist by then while for billions of years more the universe will continue to expand until the second law of thermodynamics exhausts its energy or it reverses upon itself to become a singularity. Cosmology is not philosophy but it has philosophical implications.

The Earth, we now know, is an infinitesimally tiny dot in a spiral galaxy, a swirl of stars we call the Milky Way. Life on Earth has lasted quite a long time—3.8 billion years— but *Homo sapiens* has existed for only 200,000, and the way we are going we are destroying the only world we have or will ever have. Some species of mayfly live as adults only for a day. That is us in cosmological terms, and not even a day or hours but seconds.

How to cope with this knowledge? Religion, of course, provides one answer. 'For all flesh is grass, and all the glory of man as the flower of grass. The grass withereth, and the flower thereof falleth away.' So wrote Peter in his First Epistle General. It is a common enough perception, with a sting the older you get, but of course for Christianity it is not the end of the story. The universe may well be destroyed in a kind of cosmological Armageddon different from the biblical version, but the result for those who have faith will be the same. As Peter reminded the faithful in the same Epistle: 'Blessed be the God and Father of our Lord Jesus Christ, which according to his abundant mercy hath begotten us again unto a lively hope by the resurrection of Jesus Christ from the dead, To an inheritance incorruptible, and undefiled, and that fadeth not away, reserved in heaven for you.'

It is a Get Out of Life Free card, if you have faith. If, however, you come to the conclusion that the evidence points toward the materiality of the universe, with no evidence for that conveniently nebulous concept the soul (or God), then the universe is a kind of prison, even if a magnificent and immeasurably vast one, with all life ending in the lime pit of oblivion.

Meanwhile, we are here, not having asked to be born, and giving life to others generation after generation, as if it were a gift of inestimable worth. At one level you can say it is, but at another the act of procreation is a selfish act. We do it for ourselves, because having children and watching them grow into adulthood satisfies the deepest of human needs—needs which we cannot help because they are encoded in our genetic make-up as evolved animals. 'Be fruitful and multiply,' as it says in Genesis, and all of nature heard.

What to do, if you are not religious, if God or Allah is not offering a hand to pluck you from death? All human achievement—great literature, art, music, great science— is temporal and temporary, the mayfly's dance over the river of time. Celebrate the dance and our ephemerality, perhaps, while we can.

Life in New Eden

Metaphorically speaking, you might say technology arose from the Fall, its function to make life more bearable in an imperfect world, increasing in complexity from water wheels to genetic engineering which can eradicate heritable diseases. But since we are human, light-side dark-side, technology has also increased our ability to kill each other, from spears to hydrogen bombs.

More recently, technology has become the runaway invention of our ingenious minds, and the faster we explore it, the faster technology itself evolves until it becomes almost impossible to control and impossible to stop.

What its ultimate purpose is, few people bother to ask, and with good reason, because technological advance no longer has a purpose beyond itself. There are little purposes, of course—replacing petrol-driven cars by electric ones, for example—but there is no ultimate, foreseeable goal, after achieving which humans can say, 'now we have arrived'. Instead we surge forward eagerly into a wildly proliferating, but entirely indeterminate, technological future.

This is a mistake, but in evolutionary terms *Homo sapiens* might be seen as a mistake, with technology reaching into the heart of what that mistake is, for it is no longer an adjunct to humanity but the fullest expression of what we are.

I would like this not to be so. I would like to say that

great art, poetry, fiction, music and scientific understanding fulfil this function, but this is a self-serving myth. The vast majority of humans care nothing about the arts or science, but they do care about Facebook, iPhones, cars, the latest app—technology sealing them off increasingly from the Earth as it is. Eden was conceived as a walled garden from which humanity was expelled. Turned out in a hostile world, we have at last succeeded in creating New Eden, a pixilated environment that has become reality for many.

This is in the wealthy nations, of course. For the poverty-stricken and starving who form the world's majority, it is a question of survival, of getting through another day. They can only look on with envy at the play-children of New Eden who are 'Distracted from distraction by distraction,' as T.S. Eliot wrote in *Burnt Norton*, 'filled with fancies and empty of meaning...'

Mr Zimmerman and Mr Jones

The 'Ballad of a Thin Man' on Bob Dylan's 1965 album *Highway 61 Revisited* has a refrain which everyone knows or used to know: 'Something is happening but you don't know what it is, do you, Mr Jones.' The performance is vibrant with energy, with rebellion, with scorn. The world was going to change and the young were going to make it happen. That's how it seemed, especially to students on campus who were slightly younger than Dylan. The Age of Aquarius, the Age of Love. It was always going to be summer; the young would never grow old.

I was born in the same year as Bob Dylan, was at Birmingham University through the '60s, and observed the youth movement indifferently from a distance. This had much to do with my small-town upbringing among the shopocracy.

I was never convinced by the golden youth of that decade. Its ideals were too embedded in a hedonism that could only exist in a super-rich country like America. There was the anti-Vietnam War movement, it is true, and this *did* have an impact on the US government and the course of the war. There was the civil rights movement, too, which was engaged in the serious matter of justice and rights for black Americans.

But there never was a revolution, because the movement was a *rebellion* of privileged youth and never had the revolutionary aim of seizing power and creating a new structure of government.

The Mr Joneses of middle America were certainly disconcerted and indeed they did not know what was happening. But they weren't swept away, either, any more than the deeply conservative values they lived by. The result is now all too familiar.

Toward the end of the '70s and in the early '80s there emerged a right-wing conservative counter-attack, spearheaded by Ronald Reagan and Margaret Thatcher, which succeeded because they understood the nature of political power and how to operate it.

That was the real revolution which brought in its wake the gig economy, the weakening of unions and their power to negotiate workers' rights, the decline of heavy industry, the undermining of the autonomy of universities, the rise of the super-rich and a devalued underclass. It led to George W. Bush and Tony Blair, the illegal invasion of Iraq and the destabilising of the Middle East, and a twenty-year war in Afghanistan that achieved nothing. It led in the end to Donald Trump and the storming of the Capitol, and white power resentment which is by no means finished despite Trump's electoral defeat. It led to another serial liar and populist, Boris Johnson, coming to power in England, and it led to the disaster that is Brexit.

So something indeed was going on, but it was *you* who didn't know what it was, did you, Mr Zimmerman.

White Power/White Justice

Donald Rumsfeld died the other day. He should have died in prison as one of the architects of America's illegal invasion of Iraq and its extensive programme of torture.

That never happened, of course, because no one in power in the US, or the UK, will ever be brought to justice for war crimes at the International Criminal Court in The Hague.

The invasion itself was bungled, as was the occupation, leading to the catastrophic destabilisation of the Middle East. However, although the USA and its allies lost the wars in Afghanistan and Iraq, they still wield military and economic power in the world. The International Criminal Court only prosecutes war criminals like Radovan Karadzic, Charles Taylor, and Thomas Lubanga Dyilo. It will never try an American politician or general, nor an English one. The ICC represents white power's selective justice.

Defeat and Lies

Kabul has fallen to the Taliban. The US easily drove them out of government twenty years ago and believed they had destroyed the movement, allowing George W. Bush to switch his attention to Iraq and Saddam Hussein. He was disastrously wrong.

After a twenty-year war the US and its NATO allies are pulling out amid scenes reminiscent of the fall of Saigon, as many have noted.

Biden is heavily criticised for his decision to withdraw, but if US forces stayed for another twenty years, the result would be the same.

Johnson, too, has been criticised for not 'taking over' from the Americans at Kabul Airport. This is Cloud Cuckoo thinking. British forces were defeated in Helmand; they were defeated in Basra. The British Army has lost its puffed-up reputation as 'The Best Little Army in the World'. Without American support, a small British contingent would be powerless. Once the US withdrew, British and other NATO forces had to do so as well.

On Sky News last night, the father of a Scottish soldier killed in Afghanistan was interviewed. He said his son had died for nothing. Boris Johnson said British soldiers had not died in vain.

A TV documentary last night recreated George W. Bush's movements on the day of the Twin Towers attack, from an early morning jog, to a visit to a primary school where he was told of the attack, to the growing panic among his aids who bundled the president onto Air Force 1 and flew him from air base to air base, until eventually Bush insisted on flying back to Washington, where he prepared to address the nation from the Oval Office.

As he waited to go on air, Bush suddenly slapped the flat of his hand—*bang!*—on the polished surface of the desk, and brushed something off with a flick of a finger. 'Fly,' he said.

Toward the end of the film, a voice off-screen asked if, looking back, he had any regrets about the decisions he made after 9/11. No, he said, none—he had made the right decisions, meaning the invasions of Afghanistan and Iraq. Three thousand Americans died in the Twin Towers, tens of thousands of Afghanis and Iraqis died as a consequence of the US occupations. He had made the right decisions, despite America being engaged in, and losing, a twenty-year war in Afghanistan and destabilising the Middle East for the foreseeable future.

After the 9/11 documentary, it was time for the News and we watched Joe Biden give a press conference. So far in his presidency, he has cultivated a wise old grandfatherly mien—a man you can trust, his language measured, his eyes kindly. But last night he talked tough. America will hunt down and kill Al Qaida and ISIS operatives whenever and wherever they are found. The US will do this through surgical drone strikes, like the one which recently blew up a car packed with explosives—so the Americans claimed—on its way to Kabul airport.

The trouble is, there is no such thing as a surgical drone strike. When the car was destroyed by a rocket, ten innocent Afghanis were killed as well, including six children. A US government spokesperson said they probably died when the explosives in the car blew up, with the implication that it wasn't caused directly by the rocket—if the suicide bombers hadn't packed the car with explosives, the children would still be alive. But the strike took place in a crowded suburb. The attack was never going to be 'surgical', even if the car had not carried a bomb.

The incident highlighted what we already knew, that Afghan and Arab life is cheap to the Americans, just as Palestinian life is cheap to the Israelis, America's close allies. During World War II in the Balkans, the Wehrmacht regularly shot 100 villagers for every German soldier killed by the partisans. That is roughly the ratio of Gazans who are killed whenever there is a rocket attack on Israel. In the wars in Afghanistan and Iraq the ratio is the same, if not higher. For America and its allies, life in such distant places is like the fly crushed under Bush's hand.

Last night on Sky News, a journalist was shown around the prison at Bagram Airbase in Afghanistan. There were cages where 30 men were held at a time, with steel mesh ceilings where guards could look down on them; cells where individuals could be kept in utter darkness; where prisoners were chained by their hands to the ceiling and beaten and tortured. It was a devilish place, like the prisons of Nazi Germany and Soviet Russia. Many prisoners were never charged with a crime; many were innocent. America claims to be a beacon of democracy and freedom. This is the Great Lie it tells itself.

Yesterday an American military spokesman admitted at a news conference that the drone strike in Kabul which killed a suicide bomber and 10 innocent bystanders had been a 'mistake'. The driver of the car was not a terrorist and the 'bomb' in the back of the car had probably been water bottles. The number of children killed had been updated from 6 to 7. The spokesman apologised. Relatives of those killed would be compensated with cash payments. Biden, who boasted of the 'surgical strike' when it happened, had said nothing as of last night.

A surgeon who made such an error would be struck off. America apologises, offers money, moves on. If you live in Afghanistan, Iraq, Syria, Iran, expect a surgical drone strike near you soon.

19/8 –18/9/2021

The Flaw

Colin Powell died last week. He had the makings of a tragic protagonist out of Shakespeare—a decent man who achieved high position in the Army, whose ambition tempted him to climb higher still in George W. Bush's administration. But that administration was lawless, sweeping aside the laws of war in its invasions of Afghanistan and Iraq, promoting torture at prisons in those countries and at 'black sites' in Poland, Egypt and elsewhere. Powell should never have accepted the post of Secretary of State. He was despised as weak by Rumsfeld, Cheney and Wolfowitz and kept out of key decision-making processes, but he was a useful tool and made the fatal error of presenting the case for Saddam's possession of 'weapons of mass destruction' before the United Nations. The evidence was fake, and you could tell from Colin Powell's face and body language that he knew it. At that moment Powell lost his honour. Perhaps he thought he could work with people like Cheney and Rumsfeld and not be tainted. It was a fatal miscalculation. Powell's was a modern tragedy, however, in which the protagonist did not die as a consequence of his actions. Tens of thousands of Afghanis and Iraqis did.

25/10/2021

Learning from Conrad

For many years now I have read and re-read Joseph Conrad's novels and stories. Partly this is because he is a great poet, generating metaphor and simile that stir and excite the mind, but also because the philosophy of life underpinning the fiction appeals to me. In fact, I can no longer distinguish between perceptions of mine that find an echo in Conrad and perceptions in the novels that find an echo in me. I have often thought it would be interesting to gather Conrad's observations in a pamphlet of twenty pages or so. They would not provide a coherent philosophy because Conrad was not a philosopher, but collectively they would form a conglomerate around a pessimistic and stoic view of life to which I subscribe. Here are some I have collected and noted down over the years:

'Man on this earth is an unforeseen accident which does not stand close investigation.' (*Victory*)

'I thought his memory was like the other memories of the dead that accumulate in every man's life,—a vague impress on the brain of shadows that had fallen on it in their swift and final passage.' (*Heart of Darkness*)

'Few men realise that their life, the very essence of their character, their capabilities and their audacities, are only the expression of their belief in the safety of their surroundings.' (*An Outpost of Progress*)

'It was one of those dewy, clear, starry nights, oppressing our spirit, crushing our pride, by the brilliant evidence of the awful loneliness, of the hopeless obscure insignificance of our globe lost in the splendid revelation of a glittering, soulless universe.' (*Chance*)

'No human being could bear a steady view of moral solitude without going mad.' (*Under Western Eyes*)

'What makes mankind tragic is not that they are the victims of nature, it is that they are conscious of it.' (Letter to R.B. Cunninghame Graham)

'One is sceptical of the future. For, indeed, I ask myself, why should anyone have faith in it? And why be so sad? A little illusion, many dreams, a rare flash of happiness; then disillusion, a little anger and much pain, and then the end—peace! That is the programme, and we have to see this tragi-comedy through. We must resign ourselves to it.' (Letter to Marguerite Poradowska)

'Droll thing life is—that mysterious arrangement of merciless logic for a futile purpose. The most you can hope from it is some knowledge of yourself—that comes too late—a crop of unextinguishable regrets.' (*Heart of Darkness*)

'It is only when our appointed activities seem by a lucky accident to obey the particular earnestness of our temperament that we can taste the comfort of complete self-deception.' (*The Secret Agent*)

'It's extraordinary how we go through life with eyes half shut, with dull ears, with dormant thoughts. Perhaps it's just as well; and it may be that it is this very dullness that makes life to the incalculable majority so supportable and welcome.' (*Lord Jim*)

'What is this life? Phew! Nobody can remember one-tenth of it.' (*The Rover*)

'There are occasions when the irony of fate, which some people profess to discover in the working out of our lives, wears the aspect of crude and savage jesting.' (*Freya of the Seven Isles*)

'Suicide, I suspect, is very often the outcome of mere mental weariness—not an act of savage energy but the final symptom of complete collapse.' (*Chance*. I know this to be true from the suicide of my oldest friend, Roynon Collings.)

'…it is my belief no man ever understands quite his own artful dodges to escape from the grim shadow of self-knowledge.' (*Lord Jim*)

'When once the truth is grasped that one's own personality is only a ridiculous and aimless masquerade of something hopelessly unknown the attainment of serenity is not very far off.' (Letter to Edward Garnett)

'It is, I believe, generally admitted that the dead are glad to be at rest.' (*The Arrow of Gold*)

The Meaning of a Book

I am a collector by instinct, and when I come across a writer who means a great deal to me I set out to buy his or her books in first or near-first editions. There is something about reading a work in the format in which it first appeared, because the design, the paper, the font, are all part of its original meaning, bringing you closer to how it would have been experienced at the time. Reading *Victory* in the edition of 1915 is a very different proposition to reading it in a Penguin paperback where design, paper and print reflect modern taste, a modern sensibility, which imposes a subtle distance between you and the tale.

The best examples I know of this are Caradoc Evans's *My People* and *Capel Sion*. The original editions published by Melrose, as pointed out by John Harris, were very carefully designed. The font is large, there is generous leading, and space around the text. Partly this was done to expand the books because Caradoc Evans's stories are quite short. Then there is the thick paper and the handsome maroon boards which make the collections a pleasure to handle and give them a sense of gravitas. Reading them in a modern paperback is disappointing by contrast. The stories appear to be dwarfed and somehow less significant. The words are the same, so you may argue that this is an illusion, but the book as object is part of its meaning, and that meaning is subtly changed as later editions come and go.

If you are lucky to have a signed copy that, too, brings you closer in an indefinable way to the author. I have two books signed by the Swedish poet Harry Martinson, including a first edition of his great poem *Aniara*; and one signed by Conrad, *Notes on My Books*, published in New York in 1921 in a limited edition of 250 signed copies, mine being no. 11. And there it is, in blue ink, in his distinctive hand, the large, almost circular 'C' in 'Conrad' crossed through diagonally from left to right.

I would have liked to have had R.S. Thomas's signature in one of his books. I had several opportunities to ask him but he seemed austere about such things, so I never dared. Others did, though, and on several occasions I watched as he leaned forward to autograph a title page. What I do have is a small collection of letters and cards which he wrote to me at *Planet*, and I have his unmistakable signature there.

I have a letter, too, by the Swedish novelist Per Olof Sundman, whose work I greatly admire. It was written near the beginning of his career to the editor of the Stockholm daily *Expressen*, in which he explains the aesthetic principle behind his fiction. It was advertised for a long time by an antiquarian bookseller in Sweden. Sundman is out of favour, however, because of the revelation after his death that he had been involved as a teenager in the Swedish Nazi movement, and even continued to be for a while after the war ended.

The adult Sundman supressed this, becoming a respected democratic politician as well as a much-praised novelist and short story writer. Had he come clean about his past as Günter Grass did in old age, things might have been different, but he didn't, and his reputation suffered.

Because of this, no doubt, no one in Sweden seemed to want the letter and so after it had been listed on the bookseller's website for a couple of years, I bought it myself. I re-read Sundman's fiction again and again because he is important to me and I have collected all his books in original editions, something which in fact has not been easy because his fall from grace seems to have 'disappeared' his books from antiquarian booksellers' lists.

Sundman is too good a writer to be banished to outer darkness forever, and those who now feel morally outraged by his Nazi youth conveniently forget his many years in politics working tirelessly for the cause of social democracy. The letter provides important insights into his fiction and I value the temporary ownership of it. One day, though, I will have to return it to a library in Sweden, where it belongs.

The Freedom of Being Someone Else

I have lived my adult life between two worlds, belonging to neither. One I was born into, the world of small-town shopkeepers. In my family there was a confectioner (my father), a barber-cum-tobacconist, a newsagent, a baker, and a general store owner. This world was conservative with both a lower case and a capital C; its opinions were those of the *Daily Express* and the *Daily Mail*. If it was narrow it was also safe. I belonged to it as a child, and for the most part I was happy.

I was educated into the other world. It began in sixth form with a charismatic master introducing me to literature which led to the study of English at Birmingham University. There I was thrown into high powered discussion of literature which I was ill prepared for. Lecturers and professors naturally knew a great deal more than me, but so, it seemed, did my fellow students. It was my first introduction to middle-class England. No doubt there were others who felt out of place as well, though some adapted with amazing speed. One was from a working-class family in Chester but came to Birmingham fully-fashioned, as it were, by Chester Grammar School, complete with a salt-and-pepper three-piece suit, a tightly furled umbrella, wide reading, and a good approximation to a middle-class English accent. Another who I got to know as a postgraduate, came from Durham where his father was an engine driver. He too crossed the class line with apparent ease.

It seemed that a choice could be made, if you had the confidence endowed by a high-class grammar school education. My grammar school, King Henry VIII's, was small and bedded down nicely in a small-town environment. Raymond Williams, of course, went there a generation before me, and judging from his autobiographical novel *Border Country*, suffered the same kind of disjunction at Cambridge which I was about to undergo at Birmingham, though I expect he managed it better.

I could not wait for each university term to end, boarding the train, travelling down along the border to Hereford, watching until the Black Mountains came into view, then the jarring of brakes as the train slowed to a halt at Abergavenny Monmouth Road station.

Back home I felt safe again, but education was levering me out of this world. Two friends, brothers who lived up the road, were at Oxford, and they were the only ones I could talk to about literature, jazz, blues, film, when we met during the vacations. There was less and less I could discuss with my parents, or with my cousins who I had always been close to, and I felt increasingly alienated from the world that had formed me.

The solution grew upon me unawares. I became an actor, playing a part when I went out with my cousins for a drink, when friends of my parents came round to the house in the evening for coffee and a game of whist.

And I played a part in Birmingham, too. Pretending I fitted in to an academic world where everyone was articulate and clever, learning that silence was best, contributing nothing in seminars and as little as possible in tutorials.

After a mediocre BA, and a Dip Ed which convinced me that school teaching was not for me, I returned to Birmingham and studied for an MA and a PhD, after which I obtained a post at the University of Copenhagen and taught there for thirteen years, playing the role of 'lecturer'.

I still longed for Abergavenny, and over the years honed my role as someone from the town who could hold his pint with the best of them. I believe it was a good performance, though I never discovered how many were fooled.

For forty-five years I have written, or tried to write, poems. It is the most important pursuit in my life, but I would never call myself 'poet'. It would be embarrassing, setting myself up. If anyone asks, I say I am 'scribbling this and that', and the subject is dropped. 'Poet' is a role I have never attempted.

My life as 'actor' explains, perhaps, why I have become quite a good ventriloquist, inventing characters who speak in different voices and dialects. There is a freedom in being someone else, and while I am in role, I fully believe in my characters' existence. It is as if they are real and I the pretence. They rarely venture beyond the house, however, and are generally unknown.

The Monk and the Rag-and-Bone Man

Ezra Pound saw what was essential in *The Waste Land* and cut through the dross, making it the great poem it is. Only a true poet could do that. But he was also a brow-beater, a delusionist, an obsessive, an obscurantist, stuffing *The Cantos* with Douglas's Social Credit, a hotch-potch of history, Chinese characters, quotations in Greek, Latin, Provençale, and anything else that came into to his head. Some passages are marvellous, but then you are plunged again into the impossible jumble of Pound's mind. Gertrude Stein famously called him 'a village explainer', adding 'excellent if you are a village, but if not, not', and that has him exactly.

Eliot owed a great debt to Pound and it seems to me he allowed that debt to override critical judgement when he published batches of the *Cantos* at Faber's, without editorial intervention to judge from correspondence with Pound in the 1930s. The *Cantos* needed the same drastic pruning as *The Waste Land*, but did not get it.

Eliot and Pound were remarkably successful at publicising the aesthetic that drove their own work and that of James Joyce, so much so that a whole generation of academic scholars in the 1940s and '50s took up the cause of Modernism, promoting it in book after book and making it the cornerstone of twentieth-century literature in English departments in the USA and England. The Bloomsbury group, sometimes allied with the Modernists, had a similar success, and literary history has been written in the light they shone on themselves.

It is a fact, though, that I have never met anyone who has read the *Cantos* from cover to cover, nor *Finnegan's Wake*, and I have been surprised by how many are willing to admit in private that they never finished *Ulysses*.

Recently I reread Eliot's *Four Quartets*, spurred by the reading of Volume 9 of his *Letters* covering the years 1939-41 just as the last of the quartets were being published. I am prejudiced in my reading of them because of my atheism. When I was young, though, *Four Quartets* induced in me a sense of awe. There were wonderful lyrical passages which I understood and enjoyed, but these were succeeded by meditations, on time among other things, which claimed a profundity, and had what might be called a mystical density, which I could not fathom at all.

This of course is where the academics stepped in, annotating, elucidating, and teasing out what these passages mean. Reading responses to the *Quartets*, however, from Eliot's friends and colleagues (reproduced in footnotes to the *Letters*), it is noticeable how many steered clear of venturing an opinion on the poems' deeper meaning, or meanings.

In my twenties I concluded that my failure to understand was due to my limited intelligence. Rereading the *Quartets* now, my sense is that I had been conned and that these passages convey a pseudo-profundity which says little about the nature of reality:

Time present and time past
Are both perhaps present in time future,
And time future contained in time past.
If all time is eternally present
All time is unredeemable.

'Perhaps' gives the game away here. *Perhaps* time present and time past are *not* present in time future, and *perhaps* all time is *not* eternally present. Even if it were, to say that 'all time' is 'unredeemable' is meaningless. This is a card sharper dealing from a marked deck.

My reading in evolutionary biology and palaeoanthropology over the past thirty years has no doubt also influenced me in this reaction. My impression is that Eliot knew very little science, and perhaps cared even less.

He was certainly more than a Poundian village explainer, but when he wrote *Four Quartets* he had become a sort of a retro-monastic figure whose mysticism was hammered out within the enclosed walls of Christian tradition. He would have been at home in the company of St Anselm, but rather out of his depth in the world of Darwin and T.H. Huxley.

The Waste Land remains one of my favourite poems, and one of the great poems of the first half of the twentieth century, but while Pound was a rag-and-bone man tossing on his cart anything that came to hand, Eliot increasingly dwelt in a scriptorium of the mind while the world passed by.

Negative Capability

The internet has abolished Keats's Negative Capability, 'when a man is capable of being in uncertainties, Mysteries, doubts, without any irritable reaching after fact & reason.' He gives Coleridge as an example. Coleridge 'would let go by a fine verisimilitude caught from the Penetralium of mystery, from being incapable of remaining content with half knowledge.'

Keats was thinking primarily in terms of the poet. 'This pursued through Volumes,' he concluded, 'would perhaps take us no further than this, that with a great poet the sense of Beauty overcomes every other consideration, or rather obliterates all consideration.'

Keats is right. Poets think in metaphor and symbol, they think in rhythm, assonance and alliteration. Quite often I change a line for purely aesthetic reasons and in the process may change the line's meaning. It doesn't matter so long as the revision adds to the beauty, to the 'rightness', of the line. The poet, you may say, is involved in a dance with the poem. There is no ulterior motive, no end in sight, other than the dance, and if the poem dances truly then it is also true, in the sense Keats meant in the last lines of 'Ode on a Grecian Urn' spoken by the urn:

'Beauty is truth, truth beauty,—that is all
Ye know on earth, and all ye need to know.'

Appropriate Anger

Philip Larkin who fulminated against the '3 P's', Pound, Picasso and Charlie Parker, was part of a conservative backlash against Modernism in the post-war years. Writers like him and Kingsley Amis were politicly Conservative, too—snide, petty Little Englanders, who scorned foreigners and foreign languages, and hated blacks. They were also resolutely anti-intellectual. Had they been alive in 2016 they would have voted to leave the European Union. There is much to dislike in Philip Larkin.

Despite all this, he was a very good poet, and while Late Modernists like Geoffrey Hill produced poetry that appealed to academics because it was dense to the point of incomprehensibility, Larkin wrote poems with a brilliant clarity in verse that was traditional and therefore recognisable—and yet not entirely traditional, because he used these forms to create something entirely unique to himself.

In the early 1980s I tutored a course on Modern Poetry for the Open University in Cardiff. At the time I was taken up with Ted Hughes and in one seminar disparaged Larkin by comparison. One student became extremely angry. He was a clerk of some kind in the Civil Service, with a dead-end job and no prospects. Poems like 'Mr Bleaney' spoke to him, he said, because they expressed exactly the desperation of trapped, ordinary lives, the lives of people like him. I was taken aback. The man was in his late thirties. I liked him and we got on well, but my dismissal of Larkin triggered his anger because he felt I was disparaging him, too.

I have never forgotten that encounter and have deeply regretted it for years, because I came to realise he was right. Larkin's poems are, in that rather lame word, accessible. They are written in Wordsworth's 'real language of men' and express real lives. I would like to meet my student again and explain how I have changed my views, and to apologise, but after all these years I cannot remember his name, though I do remember his face and his voice. Has anyone got angry in the same way in defence of Geoffrey Hill? I doubt it.

Varieties of Criticism

There are two kinds of literary criticism: reviews in magazines like the *LRB*, *TLS* and *New York Review of Books* which inform the reader about newly published books and provide a critical opinion on them; and academic criticism published in learned journals and monographs from university presses.

The former might be termed useful criticism. It is for the most part ephemeral but a valuable guide to what is new. I often buy a book on the strength of a review especially if it is by a reviewer whose work I know and trust.

Academic criticism is different. Driven by whatever theory of literature is in fashion, it is academics talking among themselves. One of its main functions is to further careers by fulfilling publication quotas. It is very difficult to get published unless you subscribe to the dominant theory and utilise its jargon. Criticism of this kind is therefore generally esoteric, often unreadable, and of no interest to the general reader.

For a brief period between the 1930s and 1960s there was another kind of criticism, exemplified by F.R. Leavis and A. Alvarez. This was well written in an accessible style. Works like Leavis's *D.H. Lawrence: Novelist* and *New Bearings on English Poetry* were part of a literary debate that went well beyond academia. In a similar vein, Alvarez used his position as poetry editor and critic for *The Observer* to create a taste for poets who were emerging in the early 1960s, above all through his anthology *The New Poetry* (Penguin, 1962) with its influential introductory essay 'The New Poetry, or Beyond the Gentility Principle', which was widely read. Criticism of this kind inevitably becomes historical, but *New Bearings* and 'The New Poetry' can still be read with pleasure for their style and their literary insights.

There is also a form of writing which is not criticism as such, but which has a bearing on it. This might be called poets explaining how they work. The *locus classicus* is Wordsworth's 'Preface' to *Lyrical Ballads*, followed by Shelley's *A Defence of Poetry* and the letters of Keats. T.S. Eliot's 'Tradition and the Individual Talent' is a twentieth-century example, as is Ezra Pound's 'A Retrospect'. A section of Louis Simpson's memoir, *North of Jamaica*, is the best insight into what poetry means and how it becomes that I know.

Then there is literary history and biography. As time passes, an introduction to the world in which a poet or novelist wrote can deepen the reader's understanding. Biography, which is a specialised kind of history, does this too, though in some academic circles this is denied: the author, it is claimed, is 'dead'; there is only the 'text' and the penetrating mind of the academic theorist. Interpreting a work through the writer's life, or seeking to identify the author's intention, is anathema. The shallowness and arrogance of these claims are self-evident.

When I was an undergraduate, I read a great deal of criticism. The degree course in English Literature at Birmingham University was very demanding. Students were expected to read hundreds of pages a week. I am a slow reader, and at the time felt very insecure in my own judgement. So I fell back on criticism to help me out. The trouble was I came to see Pope, or Swift, or Wordsworth, through the eyes of the critic. My experience was *mediated*, it was not my own.

When I taught at Copenhagen University I continued to read criticism, but after I left academia I gave it up. I read reviews, as I say, but the thought of an academic paper or monograph makes me groan. Relying on my own judgement means, no doubt, I miss nuances, but I gain the pleasure of immersion in the worlds of, say, Katherine Mansfield, or R.S. Thomas, and in the play of language which makes these worlds dance.

Cloud Shadows

Reading Madelaine Böhme's *Ancient Bones* has been a revelation about many things, among them the uniqueness of the human hand, its complexity and sensitivity; no other animal has evolved a hand like ours.

Then there is her challenge to the Out of Africa 1 hypothesis. Stone tools circa 2.6 million years old discovered in China, and tools of nearly the same age from India, are similar to primitive Oldowan tools found in East Africa and thought to have been produced by *Homo habilis*, the earliest accepted member of the genus *Homo*. If the dating of the Chinese and Indian finds is correct, then the scenario in which *Homo erectus* was the first human species to exit Africa about a million years ago cannot be right.

On top of this, remains of a species of great ape found in Greece, dated to c. 7 million years BP, is a good contender for the last common ancestor of chimpanzees and humans, and fossil footprints found on Crete, c. 6 million years old, are those of a bipedal species with many features resembling the human foot, though lacking crucial elements such as an arch. These predate the earliest footprints found in Africa by 3 million years.

Madelaine Böhme is also a palaeoclimatologist, however, and for me one of the fascinations of her book is her account of climate change during the past 10 million years or so. There was the Messinian Salinity

Crisis 5.6 million years ago, for example, when the narrow straits (there were two of them) connecting the Mediterranean to the Atlantic became blocked and the Mediterranean dried out, leaving salt deposits in some places two miles deep, and a canyon where the Nile disgorged into the Mediterranean basin that was deeper than the Grand Canyon today. This silted up when the basin was flooded once again as a result of a new opening to the Atlantic, where the Straits of Gibraltar are today, but geologists have been able to identify its outlines and calculate its depth.

Climate is changing all the time and has profound effects on life on Earth. We know this, or at least palaeoclimatologists and palaeontologists do, but at the same time we want to ignore it because our species has been on Earth for such a short time span that the world we have inherited seems timeless and unchanging. Hence the panic about human-induced climate change now.

The Earth has been in an interglacial period for the past 10 thousand years and eventually there will be a renewed period of glaciation when the global temperature will cool and large areas in the northern hemisphere, now heavily populated, will become uninhabitable. Many densely populated coastal regions will become uninhabitable before that, of course, as sea levels rise in response to human-induced global warming. But while global warming may delay the next ice age, there appears to be no doubt as to its eventual return.

We need to stall, if not reverse, the current trend of

global warming because its continuation will be disastrous for our species. Seen from the perspective of geological deep time, however, the Earth has been here before. Our desire to forestall the catastrophe threatening our species, and many others, is understandable, but the Earth is constantly undergoing change—20,000 years ago, sea levels were 400 feet lower than they are today and there was dry land between Wales and Ireland, and England and France.

Our lives and our reality are like watching cloud-shadows sweep across the hills, one after another, chased by sunlight, as I used to watch them in the Black Mountains when I was a child.

Men of Destiny

It is tempting in the West to look on democracy as the ultimate form of government. All peoples aspire to it, we tell ourselves, because it is the fairest form of government humanity has devised. The Americans even invade countries, as they did Iraq, to bring 'freedom and democracy' to its oppressed people, or so they said; and whatever its shortcomings democracy, when it works, does indeed stand on the principles of the rule of law, free elections, and a measure of equality for all.

I am beginning to wonder, however, whether democracy is a form of government and social organisation which is dependent on a nexus of conditions that in reality no longer exist, and that instead of being a beacon of hope for humanity, it has become a candle guttering in the dark.

With the exception perhaps of the Scandinavian nations, democracy is shifting on its foundations and may collapse in the next thirty or forty years. The assault on it comes from many directions, but the most pernicious threat comes from the triumph of global capitalism in the 1980s, engineered by Ronald Reagan and Margaret Thatcher and subscribed to by every Western government since. There is simply no alternative, we are told; it is the best for everyone. It is true that global capitalism provides the West with an abundant food supply, cheap clothes, cheap air travel to exotic destinations, but it does so at enormous cost that has to be factored in—not least the way in which the

IMF and the WTO have impoverished emerging ex-colonial nations in Africa and elsewhere by making financial loans dependent on the adoption of capitalist structures in agriculture, for example, that are entirely inappropriate to the needs of the people, while strengthening the hegemony of the West.

At home, Reaganism/Thatcherism has meant relentless deregulation and the selling off of state assets—the Royal Mail, the railways, utilities, even prisons—creating huge opportunities for speculators. Post-Thatcher, everything has been for sale, and that has included politicians, for there is a porous membrane between big business and Westminster, with ex-ministers reappearing on boards of directors, valued for their continued access to networks of political power. Tony Blair is worth an estimated £44 million, David Cameron is not far behind with £40 million. By comparison, Boris Johnson is estimated at a modest £2.9 million, though this will certainly increase now that he has left office. (Rishi Sunak, of course, outpaces them all.) Wealth, and the interface between big business and government, undermine democracy. Vast wealth equals power which seeps into the democratic system, influencing it and corrupting it. Millions of pounds are donated to the Conservative Party and in return favours are expected in the form of contracts and ultimately elevation to the House of Lords.

'All power tends to corrupt; absolute power corrupts absolutely,' in Lord Acton's well-known formulation. Substitute 'wealth' for 'power' and you have the situation of politics in America and Britain today.

One of Thatcher's most famous or infamous dicta was 'There is no such thing as society'. This is not true but Thatcher made it true in England by undermining heavy industry which was the power base of the unions and of a coherent working class. Council houses were sold off in their hundreds of thousands, denying affordable housing for those who came after, who could not buy into a housing market where prices spiralled year on year.

This policy succeeded. Today there is no working class as this has been understood for a hundred and fifty years; there are only atomised 'consumers'. Unions exist, but their influence is restricted by laws limiting their right to strike, the ultimate leverage of working men and women in dispute with employers; and the once powerful National Union of Miners was effectively destroyed when Thatcher broke the miners' strike of 1984-85.

Workers are guaranteed a minimum wage, but employers have come up with ways to undercut its cost to themselves through the 'gig economy' in which employees are offered short-term contracts or freelance work, or zero-hour contracts, thereby avoiding National Insurance payments, holiday pay, and expensive pension schemes, while maintaining effective control over an atomised workforce. In terms of employer-employee relationships it is back to the nineteenth century.

There is deepening anger and frustration among working people, but the architects of this system successfully deflected it away from themselves onto the European Union. This led to the referendum of 2016 when a campaign of lies and disinformation spearheaded by Nigel Farrage and Boris Johnson, with the support of advisers like Dominic Cummings, and powerful neo-conservative donors such as Arron Banks and Peter Hargreaves, persuaded many in the most deprived areas of the UK to vote to Leave. This is akin to shooting oneself in the head rather than the foot, but it worked, and Johnson swept into power in the 2019 general election with a massive Conservative majority.

'Take Back Control' was one of the campaign slogans in 2016, and many who voted Leave thought that was what they were doing. They were deceived. Accountable democracy is what gives ordinary people a measure of control over their and the nation's affairs, but Johnson wanted to diminish the reach of government, placing national interests de facto in the hands of large corporations and international finance. It is they who gained from Brexit, not so much taking back control but enhancing the control they already had. We have been involved in a kind of tragic pantomime, with too few to heed the shout of 'He's behind you!'

We are entering a new age of the strongman and the dictator, when libertarians take over the mechanisms of democracy in order to dismantle them one by one. It might be argued that Donald Trump was defeated at the last presidential election and Boris Johnson was eventually forced to resign. This misses the point, however, that the damage they have done lives after them. Trump may or may not get re-elected in 2024, but even if he doesn't, or doesn't even stand, almost half the US electorate believes in his values and the Republican Party has been fatally dragged to the right because it needs to retain the support of the Trumpist bloc if it is to have any chance of regaining the presidency.

In Britain the situation is complicated by the ways in which politics in Scotland and Wales have diverged from Westminster. The problem here is England where a substantial majority has a conservative mindset, as it had throughout the twentieth century, and is likely to shift further to the right as economic and social conditions worsen. In England, too, the Conservative Party shifted to the right in order to head off the threat from Nigel Farrage and UKIP. The result was Boris Johnson who has shown contempt for democratic process by his attempt to prorogue parliament in order to prevent debate of the Brexit treaty, and to 'reform' the Parliamentary Standards Committee when it found the Tory MP, Owen Paterson, guilty of breaching House lobbying rules. These are the acts of a dictatorial mind which seeks to manipulate and undermine the rule of law. The Houses of Parliament have proved strong enough to resist these raids on its authority, for the moment. The question is, for how long?

In America the situation is different: America has never been a real democracy, the Senate and Congress have always been under the direct or indirect sway of big business and finance, and of immensely influential lobbying groups like AIPAC and the NRA. The storming of the Capitol in Washington in 2021 by Trump supporters is only the beginning of a backlash by whites who feel themselves to be dispossessed. They, too, want to 'take back control' and in a nation with 270 million guns in private ownership (89 guns per 100 of the population) that is likely to be violent.

The Twisted Tree

After reading Michael Crick's biography *One Party After Another: The Disruptive Life of Nigel Farage* I've come to the conclusion that 'Britain's' exit from the European Union was not only inevitable but probably for the best. Not best for me or for many others who voted to remain, but best in that membership of the EU has been a running sore in English politics for decades, and would have remained so had the vote gone the other way, thanks to the far right in the Conservative Party, the endless stream of anti-EU propaganda from the Conservative tabloid press, and the deeply rooted delusion that 'Britain' is still a 'Great Power' which if freed from the shackles of the EU would once again take its 'rightful place' on the world stage.

Geoffrey Shepherd, my PhD supervisor at Birmingham University, used to say that historically England has alternated between periods of engagement with Europe and periods when it looked outward as an Atlantic seaboard nation. Since the eighteenth century this meant the creation and maintenance of a world empire, the source of 'Britain's' wealth and power. That empire has gone but not the sense of superiority and entitlement it engendered. The UK joined the EEC in 1973 for purely economic reasons. It never considered itself an integral part of a community of nations; it has never identified itself as 'European'.

Shortly after the referendum a meeting was held in the bandstand on the promenade at Aberystwyth. There were moving speeches in Welsh and English reaffirming our commitment to Europe. Afterwards we marched to the bar at the end of the promenade, carrying Welsh and EU flags. EU flags were being handed out and I managed to get one, holding it out fluttering in the onshore breeze. Marching back, a Scot among the bemused people on the Promenade, asked, 'Who is paying you to do this?'

There has never been another rally of the kind in Aberystwyth. It was an act of solidarity with an idea that is important, certainly, in Welsh-speaking Wales, but there was a sense of something ending that day. And this is reflected across the UK. Nearly half the electorate voted to remain in the EU, but you hear very little from them now. Power has shifted into the hands of far-right Conservatives. We live in a cruder, brasher world, with Johnson, and now Truss, on the bridge of a Ship of Fools, sailing no one knows where.

The Conservative Party, deeply corrupt, contemptuous of democratic principles and the rule of law, may get voted out at the next general election because of rising inflation which is hitting people hard. A moderate centrist government may be formed under Keir Starmer. The inherent conservatism and parochialism of the English, however, mean, almost certainly, that Starmer will be able to achieve little and will be defeated at the following general election. The political system has been twisted at its roots by people like Johnson and Farage and the tree is unlikely to grow straight again for many years, if at all.

On the Brink

Putin is getting his way, gambling on the West's indecisiveness and reluctance to become involved militarily in Ukraine. He appears to have two objectives, to prevent Ukraine from joining NATO, and to re-incorporate Donetsk and Luhansk into the Russian Federation, and perhaps, too, to overthrow Zelenskyy's government and install a puppet regime.

There is a problem in that two thirds of these provinces are still in Ukrainian hands. 'Peace keeping' Russian troops are already in the breakaway self-declared republics, however, and part of the gamble must be that the Ukrainian government will eventually cede the whole of Donetsk and Luhansk to avert the threat of a full-scale Russian invasion and a devastating war which Ukraine would lose.

If Ukraine tries nevertheless to defend what it holds of these provinces, the Russians are likely to force the issue, claiming Ukrainian provocation which will be the excuse for a limited blitzkrieg until it reaches the provinces' western border.

Donetsk and Luhansk will then be independent in name but silently re-incorporated into the Russian Federation.

Preventing Ukraine joining NATO is a parallel operation. Ukraine wants to join and the USA and its NATO allies recklessly defend its right to do so. Recklessly because Russia's anxiety about invasion from the West is perfectly understandable. The USA can protest as much as it likes that of course the West has no aggressive intentions toward Russia. If I were Putin, watching Russia progressively surrounded by NATO forces, I would not believe it. There is a new Cold War underway, and the West bears much of the blame for it.

So Putin's strategy is both defensive and aggressive. It is reasonable for Russia to want to create some kind of cordon sanitaire along its borders with the West. It is not reasonable to plot to weaken and carve up an independent Ukraine, seizing the Crimea by force, and now slicing out Donetsk and Luhansk which may not be the end of it, because Ukraine is considered an integral part of the Greater Russian Empire which it seems Putin would like to recreate piecemeal, stealing here, stealing there, testing all the while the resolve of America and the West.

At the moment he holds the best hand in this game for high stakes, because the West will not go to war over Ukraine, and Putin knows this. Severe sanctions would undoubtedly affect the Russian economy, but they would also cause Russia to look further to the East, to create stronger and deeper ties with Xi Jinping's China. Western democracies look weak and flabby when viewed from Moscow.

23/2/2022

So it was to be invasion after all, despite Putin's denial that he had any such intention. The mask has been dropped and the truth revealed. Putin says the invasion is not aimed at civilians, who will not be targeted. But in modern war civilians are *always* targeted.

25/2/2022

Putin appeals to the Ukrainian army to overthrow the government. He, Putin, could come to an agreement with the army but not with the 'drug addicts and Nazis' who run the country. We know this kind of talk from the Stalinist and Nazi thirties. If Volodymyr Zelenskyy is captured he will be abducted, given a show trial in Moscow and executed or disappear into the Russian prison system where no doubt he will suffer a 'heart attack'. Putin of course was a KGB man. He knows all about these things.

There is a canker in humanity. As regards *Homo sapiens* I am with Jonathan Swift and Robinson Jeffers

26/2/2022

A week into the invasion, Putin's intentions are clear—the overthrow of democracy, and the assimilation of Ukraine into the Russian Federation.

Some have predicted a long patriotic resistance similar to the Russian and American wars in Afghanistan. But this is not a comparison of like with like. Afghanistan has a warrior culture, the Mujahedeen and the Taliban had decades of experience fighting off invaders, they had one of the most rugged and inhospitable terrains on Earth for invading Ferenghi, as well as a porous border with Pakistan, and Pashtun tribes in Waziristan and elsewhere along that border who saw the fight in Afghanistan as their fight too.

Ukraine is mostly steppe, ideal tank country. It has a professional army and an army of volunteers mostly with little or no military experience. I imagine guerrilla warfare in such open countryside would be difficult to sustain, so resistance would be limited to the cities, involving hit-and-run attacks on Russian forces, barricades, fighting house to house, street by street. If that happens, Russian barbarity will know no limits and Kyiv, Kharkiv, Lviv will be reduced to ruins as Warsaw was during the uprising of 1944, because as Putin showed in Chechnya, he can be just as ruthless and destructive as Hitler.

The West will wring its hands, make condemnations, increase sanctions, supply arms to the defenders, pass resolutions at the United Nations, initiate war crimes investigations, take in refugees, but none of this is likely to restrain Putin, because he cannot turn back now without losing face.

Of course, there are other possible scenarios. There is growing popular opposition in Russia at the invasion, which the FSB for now is able to contain through mass arrests and imprisonment. This may change if the groundswell of opposition becomes overwhelming. It is also possible that the political elite will feel Putin has over-reached and will depose him, or that large numbers of Russian troops will mutiny. Nothing is certain.

3/3/2022

The Real Rogue State

In a review-article in *The New York Review of Books*, Jerry Brown notes that in the twenty years since the Twin Towers attack, wars have 'killed more than 900,000 people, displaced at least 38 million, and cost the United States an estimated $8 trillion'. Now Russia has joined in. So far over 1.5 million have been displaced in the invasion of Ukraine and the war has only just begun. How many will die, how great will be the material damage? How great the suffering and misery which can never be quantified?

America has learnt nothing from its aggressive, destabilising invasions and wars. As Jerry Brown points out, it is now gearing up for a confrontation with China for dominance in the Pacific. Brown sees war as almost inevitable, with the eventual use of tactical nuclear weapons, if not worse.

This is not to underestimate China's geopolitical ambitions to achieve hegemony in the region. It is America, however, that is engineering a Cold War because America will do anything to maintain its global dominance. Americans look in the mirror and see the Land of the Free, the Defenders of Democracy; they are 'good people' they tell themselves and so they fail to understand why in many parts of the world they are hated.

America is, in fact, a rogue state, initiating disastrous invasions of Vietnam, Afghanistan, and Iraq, using assassination as an instrument of foreign policy, propping up dictatorships and undermining elected governments wherever it pleases.

This century will not be one of peace, with the nations of the world uniting to save themselves and the planet. More likely, it will be a century of titanic conflicts and humanity will be consumed in the flames.

War Crimes and Lies

No one so far as I am aware has picked up on Johnson's lie to Parliament during Prime Minister's Questions yesterday, perhaps because he lies so often that people can no longer be bothered. Pressed on the Government's outrageous visa policy regarding Ukrainian refugees, he said that visa control had to be set in place because Britain was not in the Schengen area, unlike the rest of Europe. Ukraine, however, is not a member of the EU and so is not covered by Schengen. The EU nonetheless waived border controls to allow almost 2 million people to cross its border with Ukraine. The Conservative Government could easily do the same but in its mean-spirited way refuses.

Now, too, Britain and America are busy accusing the Russians of war crimes. There have been many, including the shelling of civilians and the bombing yesterday of a maternity and children's hospital in Mariupol. The UK and the USA committed war crimes aplenty in Afghanistan and Iraq and have never been brought to justice. They lost both those wars, but operate white man's justice and will never be prosecuted.

10/3/2022

What is a War Crime?

Although it seems clear that intra-species violence is a deep-seated trait in humans, and a function of the way we evolved over 200,000 years, it remains a puzzle that we have been unable to overcome it, to see that violence, whether between individuals or between nations, between religious faiths or between racial groups, is destructive and in almost all cases self-destructive. Again and again, humans embark on wars as an ultimate solution. Wars begin with an aggressive eagerness, the gathering of forces, of supplies, the spreading of maps, the revving of engines, the priming of rockets, warplanes quivering in the heat off runways, fuelled and armed, pilots giving thumbs-up from cockpits; the grand adventure is on.

But war never turns out as expected, even for the victors, if you can ever talk of victors. Who really 'won' the First and Second World Wars? Who 'won' the Napoleonic Wars? Nobody. Carnage, ruin, maiming, annihilation, suffering, these are the results of wars, Death flying his flag from the gutted buildings.

When I was a stamp collector, I had a brown Polish stamp which made a deep impression on me as a child. It consisted of an aerial view of Warsaw in 1945 or 1946, showing nothing but the burnt-out shells of buildings and rubble-filled streets as far as the eye could see. There were no humans. The most striking aspect of the stamp was the shadow of a large aircraft, from which I suppose the photograph was taken, superimposed on the desolation below like a stiff-winged unholy dove.

Now it is happening to Mariupol and Kharkiv, as it did to Raqqa and Falujah, as it may soon to Odessa and Kyiv. What to do, and where to go? Harry Martinson was right—evil is active, good reactive. The millions fleeing Ukraine are welcomed and given succour by Poland and other EU nations, with the shameful exception of England, and this is the other side of the human coin, how we can come together and help one another in times of great adversity. But soon, somewhere on Earth, Death will flip the coin again, dark-side, light-side, spinning in the slant of the Sun.

In 1945, 334 USAAF B-29s dropped firebombs on Tokyo killing 84,000 civilians; that same year, a single B-29 dropped the first atom bomb on Hiroshima killing 150,000. War crimes?

Americans frequently operate with a comic-strip view of the world—George W. Bush's 'Axis of Evil', for example, with Bush as Superman, defending *freedomndemocracy*. It is the world of *StarTrek* until it meets reality when wars, human suffering, and defeat follow.

This particular comic-book clash may end in the biggest war of all, nuclear Armageddon, something America rehearses endlessly in Hollywood catastrophe films where the few survivors are always Americans. Films like *Independence Day* are a kind of subliminal preparation for what is surely to come. At its heart,

American culture has both a lust for power and a death wish.

Apart from supplying a limited array of arms to Ukraine, US-led sanctions seem to be the only means available to oppose Putin's invasion. Sanctions American-style, however, are generally a form of foreign policy just short of outright war, and the global reach of America's military, economic, and financial might is such that it can force other countries to fall in line, with the threat of secondary sanctions if they refuse.

As Tom Stevenson points out in an *LRB* review, however, it is more often than not a brutal extension of American hegemony which affects the poor and the needy more than governments against whom sanctions are supposedly aimed. He gives the example of Venezuela, where US sanctions aimed at getting rid of Nicolás Maduro were the direct cause of the death of at least 40,000 people. I suppose that is not considered a war crime because the imposition of sanctions is not considered an act of war. Perhaps it should be.

I have been trying to tot up how many wars there have been in my lifetime: World War II, the Korean War, the Vietnam War, the First and Second Chechen Wars, the Russian war in Afghanistan, the American war in Afghanistan, the American war in Iraq, Israeli-Arab wars in 1948, 1956, 1967, 1973, 1982, the Iraq-Iran War, the Falklands War, three wars between India and Pakistan over Kashmir, the Russo-Georgian War, civil wars in Cambodia, Syria, Libya, Lebanon, Yemen, war in East Timor, and now the Russo-Ukrainian War. There must be others, that I never knew about, or never paid attention to.

11/3-6/4/2022

Near the Limits

The problem with humanity *en masse* is that we do not understand what we are. We think we do, but confuse the surface details of life with the deep structure shaped by the evolutionary history of our genus over three-and-a-half million years.

There are many around the world who say we are not animals. We were created by God in a unique act, distinguished from all other creatures by the possession of an immortal soul. I have met otherwise intelligent people who believe humans have always existed on Earth and can never die out—a spin-off perhaps from the biblical claim that Man was created fully-formed on the sixth day. There is no point in disputing such convictions because no evidence to the contrary will persuade believers that they are wrong.

Thanks to technological advance in the past two hundred years, we have created ever greater complexity and artificiality in the world around us, and the pace of that complexity grows exponentially as new technology opens doors on room after room filled with seeming opportunity.

Among other consequences, this has led to a global flight from the land, with small-scale agriculture increasingly replaced by agribusiness—giant plantations, giant fields serviced by a small contingent of technofarmers high in the cabins of over-sized tractors or combine harvesters. The flight from the land has created megacities which increase in size and number as the global human population continues to expand. Until the Covid-19 pandemic, I had never heard of Wuhan, yet it is a city of 10,000,000 people, and recently I heard of another city in China, whose name, even, I cannot remember, with a population of 18,000,000. Urban environments are, you might say, our ant hills or termite mounds, but on such a scale and of such ingenious artificiality that they conceal from us their origin in humanity's deeply animal nature.

Humans and chimpanzees are placed in separate genera, *Homo* and *Pan*. We nonetheless share 96 percent of our genes with chimpanzees. That 4 percent difference leading to the megacities and humanity's current global dominance, while the two species of chimpanzees are restricted to shrinking equatorial forests and are threatened with extinction.

We gaze at each other across a ravine of time and circumstance. I don't like going to zoos, but I have been several times to the Ape House at Copenhagen Zoo to watch a family of chimpanzees housed in a large enclosure, with concrete walls on three sides, the fourth being of glass where visitors like me can gaze at the inmates and sometimes they gaze back.

We are of course the only member of our genus left on Earth, though fifty or sixty thousand years ago this was not the case. At that time, we shared it with at least two, and perhaps four, other human species—*H. neanderthalensis* and *H. floresiensis*, and possibly *H. erectus* and *H. altaensis* (if the latter is indeed a separate species).

Had any of them survived into modern times, how

would we have responded? In the heyday of European colonialism in the nineteenth century they would probably have been driven to extinction, or perhaps enslaved.

Homo floresiensis, though, was tiny—three feet six inches tall which is the same height as 'Lucy', the famous specimen of *Australopithecus afarensis* who lived some 3.2 million years ago. Its brain was proportionately small—426cc, only slightly larger than Lucy's or that of a chimpanzee. By comparison, the brain of a modern human averages 1400cc. Existing only on the island of Flores in present-day Indonesia, might this hominin, so strange, so different to modern eyes, have been kept in zoos alongside chimpanzees?

We gaze through the plate glass in the Ape House across that ravine, and what do we see? In *The Chimpanzees of Gombe* Jane Goodall has described how chimpanzees are organised in extended families, taking in females from other groups for the purposes of breeding. When a group becomes too large, there is a split which is not always peaceful. In one incident, the larger, more powerful group stalked the smaller breakaway group, attacking and killing the males and capturing the females. It was war-in-embryo. In another, a female and her adult daughter wantonly killed the babies of others. Chimpanzees are mainly vegetarian, but when opportunity arises they hunt monkeys through the trees in organised bands, tearing the unfortunate monkey apart if the hunt is successful, with subordinates begging for pieces of meat from the dominant members of the group. Cannibalism also occurs, especially after a battle.

What we are looking at is the bedrock of much human behaviour. We are not chimpanzees and chimpanzees are not us, but we share these deep traits which appear again and again in hypertrophied form across human societies.

Our large brains, relative to body weight, make us far more intelligent than chimpanzees and the argument can be made that intelligence, combined with human sympathy, can counter and even overcome the deep structure of our nature. The feminist movement has substantially altered the position of women in the western democracies and how men think of themselves in relation to women, for example, though the process is incomplete and fragmentary, and is non-existent in many parts of the world. Other things do not change— the struggle for power, for wealth, and for the influence that wealth brings, socially and politically.

We have not been successful in eradicating war either. It remains often the first, not merely the last, resort in international and internecine disputes, as the war in Ukraine demonstrates.

In so many ways we say one thing—even believe one thing—yet act contrary to reason and compassion. COP26 will be followed by COP27, COP27 by COP28, but global humanity needs to unite *now* if we are to avert the multiple, interrelated catastrophes we have set in motion.

Can we access the deep structure of the human mind in such a way as to override its imperatives which not only impede, but in many ways prohibit, radical change in our behaviour? That is the question.

What Should the Study of Literature Mean?

The education I received in English literature is obsolete, though I have been reluctant to come to terms with this. Studying, as I did, at an English university in the early 1960s, the emphasis was on the canon of English literature, which was deemed to extend from *Beowulf* through Chaucer, Langland, and *Sir Gawain and the Green Knight* to a reading of the acknowledged major writers from the sixteenth to the early twentieth centuries.

As an undergraduate, I had no idea that this was quite a recent innovation in the perception of what literary studies should be in the modern world. The pre-eminence of Classical Greek and Latin literature which had remained unchallenged for several centuries had been toppled, to be replaced by the 'classics' of English literature. So instead of Homer, Virgil, Ovid, Horace, we read Milton, Pope, Wordsworth, Tennyson. The authors were different, but the underlying principle remained the same—there was a body of great writing which anyone educated in literature would need to know. There even remained a vestige of the older system. At grammar schools in the 1950s Latin was a compulsory subject, and O-level Latin a compulsory qualification if you wanted to study English literature at university level.

Universities are embedded in society. Inevitably they

change as society changes, responding to its demands and pressures. Since Thatcher, too, universities have come under increasing government scrutiny and control, directed by politicians with little interest in the humanities which can easily be dismissed as a middle-class luxury, tolerated but irrelevant to the pressing needs of a culture wedded to economic growth and the expanding horizons of a digital universe.

In 1960 it was still possible to think of England as an ethnically homogenous, class-based society with an elite, drawn increasingly from a meritocratic education system. This system operated from the top down, and the syllabus for a bachelor's degree in English was compulsory. For the finals examination at Birmingham University, where I studied, there were eight three-hour papers encompassing literature from the eighth to the nineteenth centuries. There was one element of choice in the third year when you could continue the study of Old English or opt for the early twentieth-century.

The course was gruelling, especially for a slow reader like myself, but I came away from it with a solid grounding in the historical depth of English literature. I have never read Milton since, in my second year, I was obliged to read his major poetic works in a week for a tutorial, but I retain a distinct sense of the sombre grandeur of his verse which has never left me, and which I would not be without.

2022 is a very different world, however, and the response of students and many teachers of literature is likely to be a shrug of the shoulders. Who wants to read Milton now? Or Ben Jonson? Or William Langland?

This is the twenty-first century and we are living in the 'UK', a multi-ethnic, multi-cultural world with new horizons.

Today there are all kinds of niche literatures to explore from all kinds of perspectives, so a syllabus may include courses on gay or feminist literature, or literature from ethnic minorities. To accommodate these developments, courses have increasingly become modular, based on subjects with perceived contemporary relevance which will appeal to students. The latter is important. Since Thatcher commercialised the universities, fee-paying students have become customers in a supply-and-demand system, and customer satisfaction is a prominent consideration when designing a syllabus.

The English Department at Aberystwyth University, for example, offers modules in the first year on Literature and the Sea, Contemporary Writing, An Introduction to Poetry, and Re-imagining Nineteenth-Century Literature. In 1960, 'An Introduction to Poetry' would seem a very anomalous course in an Honours BA programme. Students were introduced to poetry in sixth form at school. What the module reflects, I suspect, is that students are very resistant to reading poetry which is presented here as a niche option among others.

Re-imagining Nineteenth-Century Literature is a different kind of module again. It examines the ways in which *Pride and Prejudice*, *Jane Eyre*, and *A Christmas Carol* have been adapted and reworked. Students will study Jean Rhys's *Wide Sargasso Sea*; the Bollywood film

Bride and Prejudice, and *The Muppet's Christmas Carol* 'which has been described as the most faithful film adaptation... raising questions of what we understand by fidelity in literary adaptations' according to the course description.

Throughout the three years, there is a distinct emphasis on 'creative writing'. Indeed the English Department now styles itself the Department of English & Creative Writing, reflecting the popularity among students of what may easily appear to be a non-subject. Each module offers 'student choice', but in a controlled way, because there is a list of 'outcomes' which students can be expected to achieve if they take the course.

A degree based on this modular system offers exploratory shafts, as it were, drilled into the strata of literature and culture, mainly in England, but also more widely in the variety of literatures that exist in English around the world. It is an accurate reflection of the disarticulated culture we have now, where the young appear to be free and at home. To me it seems like trying to finish a jigsaw with pieces from different puzzles.

The cultural coherence underpinning my degree course, which provided what seemed, and still seems, a rich and deep foundation for a lifetime of reading, would be impossible now. To the young, attending university today, it is inconceivable

Approaching the Bottleneck

According to Elsa Panciroli in *Beasts Before Us*, an estimated 1 million animals a day are killed on the roads in America. Multiply that up around the world and roadkill itself will do for many species unable to breed faster than they are crushed to death.

I was pleased, if that is the word, to read that Elsa Panciroli agrees with my prediction that foremost among the species likely to squeeze through the extinction bottleneck are cockroaches and rats. Small is good, it seems, when faced with mass extinction. Large is bad. She predicts that all the megafauna of Africa and elsewhere will succumb to extinction in the wild, surviving perhaps in zoos. Humans of course are among the megafauna.

Strangers

It is summer here, and spring is coming in Ukraine. It must be easy to feel mocked by that vigorous spontaneity of life while people are encased in destruction, fear and death, or crowd on buses to leave their lives behind. Might some consider it an ultimate freedom? To be nothing more than a human being who has slewed off the skin of the past, standing alone? Perhaps, for an exceptional individual, but most drag their past with them, or try to create a new life, surrounding themselves with new things, creating new skins.

Many end up caught between two worlds, belonging to neither. My Serb landlord in Birmingham when I was a student, Radomir Stefanovic, a big man, was like a beached whale with his heavily accented English, his dreams of life before the Second World War, his awareness that he would always be that 'bloody foreigner' in the Cadbury's chocolate factory where he worked.

My friend and neighbour in Copenhagen, too, the Polish historian Emmanuel Halicz. He did not seem to linger in the past like Radomir, but nor did he, or could he, ever belong in Denmark. He and his wife Anna's flat was filled with furniture which they had been allowed to bring with them when they left Poland in the early 1970s. It was like a stage replica of a bourgeois Polish living room where actors played out the drama of being Poles.

For Emmanuel and Anna there was no way back to Communist Poland. For their two children it was different. One became a doctor living in Italy; the other a scientist who settled in Israel. After the collapse of the USSR, Emmanuel and Anna visited Poland once or twice, to find themselves strangers there because Poland had moved on.

At one level we are all strangers, to ourselves and each other, but that is territory where most do not wish to go.

The Future is Mega

A megacity is defined as a city with 10 million or more inhabitants. The largest today are Shanghai (24 million), Delhi (28 million), and Tokyo (37 million). I have only visited one, when I spent a week at a poetry conference in Istanbul, population 14 million. Seen from the air, it appeared to spread to the horizon in all directions, and the drive by taxi to the old walled city of Constantinople where my hotel lay took over an hour through dense traffic.

Constantinople, at the height of Byzantine power in the ninth and tenth centuries had a population of between 500,000 and 800,000. With its massive defensive walls and towers, and imposing palaces and churches, it was one of the wonders of the early medieval world. Today it is surrounded and diminished by the vast sprawl of tenement blocs, shopping centres, petrol stations, factories, arterial roads, needed to house and sustain its present-day population—a jewel in the head of a toad.

Copenhagen is a small city, by comparison, with a population of 1.3 million. I lived there for thirteen years and was part of its life, and we have returned every year to visit family and friends—except for the past three years when the pandemic made it impossible.

Returning this summer, I stood at the window of our airport hotel room on the eleventh floor. There was the Sound between Denmark and Sweden, one of the busiest shipping lanes in the world, with cargo ships large and small, and massive cruise liners arriving at Oceankajen to disgorge thousands of tourists. Passenger planes, too, flew in every couple of minutes to land. Goods trains moved slowly at the foot of the hotel, many waggons long. Beyond the line, was a four-lane highway, with lorries, cars, vans, buses, speeding as if time was everything and there was not enough of it.

Riding the Metro into the city centre, on driverless trains, we were packed tight with other passengers, almost all of whom had white down-pointing earphones, with iPhones never out of their hands. I glanced surreptitiously when I could at what people were looking at. Mostly it was Facebook or Twitter, scroll-scroll-pause-scroll-scroll-scroll-pause, 'distracted from distraction by distraction', as T.S. Eliot put it, though he could not have imagined the means we have at our disposal today to shield ourselves from engagement with the world around us.

What we see of a city is only its superstructure. Wherever workmen dig a trench, a mysterious tangle of pipes, cables, wires, junction boxes is revealed, their purpose entirely opaque to passers-by; and somewhere below that, the city's sewage system, its tunnels known only to the workers who maintain them, and to the rats. Somewhere far down, too, tunnels of the Metro with their thousands of rushing humans.

Cities are both highly ordered and wildly chaotic. Each inhabitant has a purpose, going about the streets with small meanings, small intentions which give coherence to individual lives. People tend to create 'villages' as well—circumscribed areas where they feel at home. Some of these *were* villages once, engulfed by the ever-expanding city. Yet these are like eddies or backwaters in the ceaseless rush of life, the reverberation of traffic echoing off walls, the power of so much kinetic energy—luxury stores—Gucci, Armani—all the foods of all the world—beautiful women and smartly dressed men—and pavement poverty, 'I am homeless and hungry. Please help'.

Many thrive on what might be called the city's chaotic order, especially perhaps if you are born to it. I taught a first-year student once at Aberystwyth University. She was from London, and deeply unhappy. She couldn't stand the fact that wherever you went in town, you could see fields and hills or the sea. She felt exposed, and longed for the comfort of endless streets, bricks and mortar, fast moving crowds, the moan and roar of traffic. I am not sure what happened to her as I only taught part-time for a term, but I would be surprised if she hadn't given up and gone home.

London's population is 9 million. It sprawls and sprawls, but is dwarfed by Tokyo which is four times the size. What would it be like living among 37 million people? I will never know, because I will never go there.

But megacities are the future, as more and more drift from the countryside, as refugees crowd and wander the world, attracted in ever greater numbers by the gravitational field of the great cities; and as the global population rises inexorably.

What to do? Nobody knows, but we are now a plague species, and evolutionary history suggests that plague species eventually destroy themselves. For the while, we are here, and the megacities grow each decade, many tens of millions of people cut off from, and ignorant of, the natural world on which all life depends. We are well on the way to creating a variant of *Homo sapiens*—a cultural subspecies, you might say—which knows nothing except the vast sprawl of megacity life, entirely dependent on high technology and believing, or hoping, that technology will solve the problems created by our overwhelming numbers.

New technologies, however, almost always have unintended consequences. A hundred years ago, the motor car offered vistas of unimaginable freedom to those who could afford it; now millions of cars pollute the cities and the countryside, dominating how we live, whether we like it or not. (Electric cars, incidentally, are no solution, they merely create other problems of their own: rare metals are needed for their batteries, and vast amounts of energy are needed to produce them, while the demand for electricity to run them will be a burden on energy supplies at a time when nations are struggling to adapt to a carbon neutral environment.)

The answer is a dirigiste ban on the private car. Then there would be no need for motorways; city and town centres would return to a slower, more restful way of life; we would breathe more freely; we would have the opportunity to be more human.

That is never going to happen, of course. Any government, whether democratic or autocratic, that tried to introduce such a ban, even gradually and through encouragement, would be finished. Car owners can think up a dozen reasons why having a car is essential to their way of life and to their freedom. Impossible, the thought that perhaps they are the slaves of car culture, not its masters.

We continue on our way, sleepwalking to the edge of the precipice, febrile yet dissatisfied, undernourished, though we couldn't quite say how, while the megacities expand across the face of the Earth, where the war of humanity against itself and against nature will be played out.

too—Thatcher, Blair, George W. Bush, Trump, Putin; and books about ISIS, the Taliban, the invasions of Afghanistan and Iraq; trying to understand the turmoil of the world in which we live and to extrapolate from it where humanity might be heading.

I would not have read such books fifty years ago, because I knew less and understood less. Moreover, reading palaeoanthropology and palaeontology has deepened my sense of time and humanity's brief place in the history of life on Earth.

Don't Be Fooled

During visits to Oxford, Copenhagen, and Reykjavík this summer, it became clear to me that within ten years or so money will disappear, to be replaced by credit card and iPhone payment. Everywhere we went, most people paid for goods and services in this way. Travelling by train, the young, especially, showed the ticket inspector their on-screen tickets, or tickets bought from a station machine. In Denmark now there are no ticket offices and while that is not so here, yet, it will come within the next few years if the rail companies have their way.

In Denmark, too, there are no longer any real post offices and Danes are encouraged to print out 'stamps' on their computers, estimating the weight and the appropriate cost of postage themselves. Parcels are not delivered to the house, but are deposited at the nearest store, usually a supermarket, for collection.

This of course is the smart future, delivered by IT companies who make huge profits from it, and eagerly seized upon by airports, airlines, rail companies, and privatised postal services, who make equally huge savings, reducing staff to a minimum, off-loading much of the work involved onto the customers.

There are, however, unintended consequences. One is that images on coins, banknotes, and postage stamps, which act as emblems of a nation's collective identity, will disappear. Denmark, for example is a land of islands and so a land of bridges, it is also a land rich in

Neolithic and Bronze Age artefacts. The 500 kroner banknote has on its obverse Queen Alexandrine's Bridge and on the reverse a Bronze Age bowl; the 100 kroner note has the old Lillebælt Bridge (obverse), with a finely worked Neolithic dagger (reverse). Sweden also celebrates antiquities on its banknotes. The reverse of the 50 kronor note has an image of Bronze Age rock carvings. Sweden tends, though, to celebrate cultural figures on the obverse. The 50 kronor note has a portrait of Evert Taube, a popular singer/entertainer of the last century; while the 200 kronor note has a portrait of Ingmar Bergman.

The UK too favours cultural ikons on the reverse of its banknotes: J.M. Turner on the £20 and Jane Austen on the £10 note. The £5 invokes English patriotism with Winston Churchill.

Postage stamps, of course, have celebrated various aspects of a nation's identity for over a hundred years in an almost endless variety.

We may not think about it consciously, but when we hand over a banknote in a shop, or attach a stamp to an envelope, a subliminal sense of one's collective identity is present. I always ask for Welsh definitive stamps at the post office and refuse English/British ones.

When money is finally phased out, people's sense of community, of belonging, will be that little bit the less. We will be a step nearer the fully atomised 'society' which is the goal of neocapitalism, because isolated people are easier to control, both as workers and as 'consumers' of the system's products. A banknote makes a statement. A credit card or an iPhone makes a statement too, but it is one of an impersonal transaction mediated by machines.

12/9/2022

Afterword

These observations were written between 2020 and 2022. They are of necessity provisional because everything is in flux, with multiple crises interacting in ways that baffle prediction.

What, for instance will be the outcome of the war in Ukraine: The partition of Ukraine? Defeat and withdrawal of the Russian forces? A resort to tactical atomic weapons by a desperate Vladimir Putin. 'Collateral damage' to the giant Zaporizhzhia nuclear power plant with consequences far worse than Chernobyl? Accidental escalation drawing the USA and NATO into a catastrophic Third World War? Or perhaps none of these things, perhaps something entirely unforeseen lurking beneath the horizon? At the time of writing, it is impossible to say.

It is the same with the climate crisis which will worsen progressively as governments worldwide fail to take sufficient steps to arrest the increase in mean global temperature. This cannot be separated from human overpopulation, because overpopulation is the ultimate cause of climate change and a host of other problems that are affecting the health of the planet.

These short essays also touch on nearer concerns: poetry, literary criticism, the fate of the humanities. Compared with the great tsunami that is gathering to overwhelm us, such concerns may seem trivial: fiddling, not while Rome, but the Earth burns. Yet the arts are, and have always been, a vital expression of who we are as a species. To set them aside now would be a mistake, a diminution of our humanity, and we cannot afford that.

What to do, then? I write poems because something in me demands it; I write essays, like these observations, out of conviction that, if we can do little else as individuals, we can at least take on the role of witness, in the sense used by old-time southern Black preachers who, in the middle of a sermon, would pause to ask the congregation, 'Do I have a witness here tonight!'